TEEN-AGE
ALCOHOLISM

TEEN-AGE ALCOHOLISM

JIM HASKINS

HAWTHORN BOOKS, INC.
Publisher/New York

CONTENTS

ACKNOWLEDGMENTS

I am grateful to my editor, Carolyn Trager, for her patience and her help; to Susan Fener for her research work; to Mary Ellen Arrington, who typed the final manuscript; and to Kathy Benson, without whom this book would not have been possible.

TEEN-AGE
ALCOHOLISM

1

FACTS AND MISCONCEPTIONS
ABOUT ALCOHOL ADDICTION

Problem drinking among young people is increasing. There are lots of studies and even more statistics to prove this statement. Some of these statistics will be given in this book, but not too many. Statistics are important, but being able to quote a number of statistics is not the same as understanding what those statistics mean. They do not help young people with drinking problems, and they are not particularly successful in supporting young people who do not want to develop drinking problems. Much more important is an understanding of what people drink, why people drink, and what people can do about problem drinking. Presently, there is a great deal of ignorance and misinformation about alcohol and drinking. Test yourself by answering true or false to the following statements:

- Addiction to alcohol is very much like addiction to heroin.
- Alcoholism is a twentieth-century problem and was not a source of concern in earlier centuries.
- Expressions such as *oiled* and *tipsy* are new ways to describe overdrinking.
- Young alcoholics are much more emotionally disturbed than adult alcoholics.

11

- Beer is less intoxicating than whiskey mixed with water.
- Strawberry, apple, and similar fruit wines are more intoxicating than beer.
- Cold showers and strong coffee will sober up a drunk person.
- The size of the body affects the amount of liquor one can hold.
- Mixing drinks can increase the effects of alcohol.
- Alcohol can make you fat and cause malnutrition at the same time.
- Alcohol is good to drink when you are cold, for it acts as a warming agent.
- Teen-agers who drive after drinking a relatively small amount have no more accidents than people aged 25–69 who drive with the same low concentrations of alcohol in their blood.
- Drinking helps sexual performance.
- Drinking when you are depressed helps you feel better.
- The alcoholic does not enjoy getting drunk.
- If you can go "on the wagon" for two weeks, you do not have a drinking problem.
- Alcoholics are easy to spot.
- The idea that an alcoholic can only kick the habit by never taking another drink again is not necessarily true.

This book examines the facts about alcohol and alcohol addiction to determine which of these statements are true, which are false, and how this information can help alcoholics and society in general to deal with problem drinking.

2

ALL ABOUT ALCOHOL

The sweetest wines may turn to the tartest vinegar.—James Howell, 1647

Alcohol is the best of all preservatives. —Percival Wilde, 1940

WHAT ALCOHOL IS

The word *alcohol* refers to a whole family of chemical compounds, not all of which are good to drink. There is rubbing alcohol, for example; also, wood alcohol and methyl alcohol. What all types of alcohol have in common are an oxygen atom and a hydrogen atom linked together in a certain way to form what is called a hydroxyl group. Depending on the construction of this group and the other atoms with which it is linked, a very poisonous substance, such as methyl alcohol, can result; or, a generally nonpoisonous type of alcohol, ethyl alcohol, can be produced. The alcoholic beverages people drink contain ethyl alcohol.

Alcohol is not a food, although it shares some of the properties of food. Like food, it contains calories, which accounts in part for the condition commonly known as "beer belly."

Unlike food, it contains no vitamins, minerals, or proteins; in other words, it contains no nutrients. People who drink a lot of alcohol often feel full, and thus they do not feel the need to eat. Alcohol *is* filling, but it is not nourishing.

The reason alcohol is filling is that it shares another characteristic of food: Like meat, fruit, or milk, it must go through the process of digestion, or oxidation. The process begins in the stomach, where the stomach muscles start a churning movement not only helps get the digestive fluids secreted by the stomach lining to the food but also gets some of the oxygen in the body to the food. The oxygen combines with the food, burns off its chemical ingredients, and turns it into carbon dioxide and water. Most foods are oxidized slowly and in successive stages, first in the stomach and small intestine, allowing the various nutrients in the food to be absorbed slowly into the bloodstream for distribution to the parts of the body where they are needed. Because of the small size of the ethyl alcohol molecule, alcohol begins to oxidize immediately. It is absorbed into the lining of the stomach and small intestine virtually unchanged in form. Instead of *being* acted upon by the stomach it acts *on* the stomach walls. Large amounts of alcohol over a period of years damage the stomach lining and cause the stomach muscles to lose tone. This means that the stomach action is slowed down, including the important churning movements involved in digestion. The stomach is no longer able to digest and expel into the intestine the entire contents of a meal. Some of the food remains undigested in the stomach, which is the main reason for the "beer belly."

After the alcohol is absorbed into the stomach and small intestine, it is carried by the blood into the liver. The liver is not equipped to handle a large amount of alcohol at one time. It must accept what it can handle and send the rest away. The alcohol sent away is unoxidized and thus remains in relatively pure form. It is carried by the blood to the heart, which in turn pumps it back into the circulatory system, where it reaches every part of the body, including the brain, and eventually returns to the liver. The liver accepts some more alcohol for oxidation and sends the rest on to the heart again. This process continues until the alcohol is completely oxidized. Meanwhile, alcohol, like actual foods, has reached every part of the body. The difference is that while real foods travel throughout the body in oxidized or digested form, alcohol passes through the various organs in unoxidized form. While the stomach and liver suffer most from excessive amounts of alcohol, no part of the body is unaffected.

Alcohol was considered a food for many years, but now it is understood that alcohol is really a drug. It differs from cocaine, heroin, or other drugs, which must be snorted, smoked, or injected, only in that it goes through the digestive system. Like the more commonly recognized drugs, alcohol acts on the central nervous system, causing certain portions of the brain to be overactive and to suppress unpleasant feelings or anxieties. Thus it is really an anesthetic. Also, like the more commonly recognized drugs, alcohol can build up a dependence. As with other drugs, this dependence is psychological at first, but then it can become physical.

Psychological dependence means that people feel they need a drug to function properly. Common examples of people who are psychologically dependent on drugs are those who cannot start the day without a cup of coffee or tea (caffeine) or those who cannot seem to digest a meal if they do not have a cigarette (nicotine) after it. Psychological dependence on alcohol is evident if a person cannot relax after a day's work without having at least one drink or cannot enjoy him/herself at a party without drinking.

Physical dependence occurs after a long period of increasing psychological dependence. Certain chemical changes actually take place in the brain cells, making it impossible for the person to function normally unless the drug is available.

Drug addiction involves two things. The first is tolerance. Through daily use of large amounts of a drug, the body adapts to it and requires more to produce the same effect. Heavy drinkers are people who now have to have six drinks in order to feel the way they used to feel after two drinks. The second characteristic of drug addiction is the reaction of the body when the drug is not available to it. We are familiar, through movies and television, with the withdrawal symptoms of people addicted to narcotics. An alcoholic deprived of drink also goes through withdrawal symptoms, called DT's, or delirium tremens—convulsions of the body and hallucinations. When a person craves alcohol and has a compulsive need for it after an extended period of heavy use, he or she is just as addicted to alcohol as a heroin addict is addicted to that drug.

HOW ALCOHOL IS PRODUCED

> What's better than the beer that's made from malt?—James Howell, 1659.

> Season the woode neuer so well the wine will taste of the caske.—John Lyly, 1579.

There are two basic kinds of alcoholic beverages, those produced by fermentation, such as beer and wine, and those distilled, such as vodka, gin, bourbon, whiskey, scotch, rye, or brandy. Of the two types, those produced by fermentation have existed much longer. In fact, beer and wine in some form have probably been around almost as long as humans have.

Only three things are needed to produce a fermented beverage: sugar, which is contained in fruits, honey, or sprouted seeds; yeast, which is carried in the air; and time. When grain or fruit is left standing for a long period of time, the yeast molecules in the air act on the sugars in the process of fermentation. This can happen naturally, as when a pile of apples is left out in a field, berries rot on a bush, or grain is stored too long. The liquid formed by yeast on grain produces beer. The liquid formed by yeast on fruit produces wine.

Thus it was probably by accident that people discovered alcohol, long before they were able to leave records to let later generations know about it. Nevertheless, what records do exist show that alcohol has an impressively long history, extending back at least 7,000 years.

Archeologists have found clay tablets from ancient times showing that as long ago as 5000 B.C. people drank beer. There are references to alcohol in India in 2000 B.C. The Bible credits Noah with discovering wine and planting the first vineyard after the Flood. The ancient Greeks and Romans enjoyed wines, as did the Aztecs, who made a beer from corn. The early Anglo-Saxons made a wine from fermented honey, which they called mead.

Beverages that we now call hard liquor were not invented for thousands of years after the discovery of beer and wine. While beverages ferment almost by themselves, humans must take a more active part in the production of distilled liquors such as scotch, gin, whiskey, rye, and others.

Distillation is a process by which a liquid is heated until it turns into a gas, which is trapped and turns into a liquid again, the impurities meanwhile having been burned away. As far as we know, distillation was first discovered around 800 B.C. The Chinese already had drinks made from fermented rice and millet, and before long they realized they could make even stronger drinks through distillation.

For those who enjoyed the effects of alcoholic drinks, this was, of course, the attraction of the distillation process. Fermented beverages can contain only a certain percentage of alcohol, because the yeast molecules can grow just so large before they stop growing and fermentation stops. With distillation, a much higher alcoholic content can be achieved. Alcohol can be distilled down to an almost pure form, and liquids of various alcoholic content can be produced, depending on how much water is added.

We have no records that the process of distillation was discovered anywhere else for another 1,500 years. In the eighth century, in Arabia, distillation was discovered by a man called Geber, who was looking for gold. Geber believed that gold could be made from other metals by subjecting them to intense heat. The heat would remove all impurities from these metals and leave only gold. One of the early modern scientists, Geber did not use heat on metals only. Before long he was using it on a variety of substances, including wine. Like the Chinese, hundreds of years before, he discovered that heating wine and burning away the impurities produced a much stronger liquor.

In those days, Arabian women put a powder on their eyelashes to achieve much the same effect as the women of today do with mascara. It was called *al-kuhul*. Geber probably decided the product he had made from heating wine looked very much like that powder, for he called it *al-kuhul*, too. Later the term became *alcohol*.

Geber worked during the eighth century. In the thirteenth century people were still trying to make gold by a variety of chemical processes. People were also looking for a medicine that would cure all diseases, and in France Arnaud de Villeneuve, a professor of medicine, rediscovered the process of distillation. He called the result of heating wine *aqua vitae*, (water of life), which was the original brandy.

The rediscovery of distilled liquor did not cause Europeans to abandon fermented beverages. In fact, they continued to improve them and to find new ones. During the Middle Ages, Christian monks were the best winemakers in Europe. Some of the finest types of wine ever produced, including champagne, were developed by monks.

Explorers from Europe found strange and delicious alcoholic drinks in the New World. Christopher Columbus's crew brought rum back to Spain. Rum was made from fermented molasses taken from sugar cane, which grew in the West Indies, and it became very popular in Spain. Later, English explorers also discovered rum, and it became the favorite drink of English sailors.

Meanwhile, other types of distilled liquor were being developed in different countries. In the middle sixteen hundreds a professor of medicine in Holland tried distilling the fermented barley out of which beer was made. The result was a bitter-tasting liquid, which we know as vodka. When the Russians discovered the liquid, vodka became the Russian national drink. The Dutch did not like the taste and added juniper berries to improve it, thus producing gin, which became the national drink of the Netherlands.

Both the Irish and the Scots made their own kinds of alcohol by distilling barley in a different way. The result was whiskey. The way the Scots cured their barley gave it a strong, smoky flavor. In fact, it was so distinctive that the whiskey made by the Scots came to be called simply *scotch*. Both rye and bourbon were invented at the end of the eighteenth century.

In the mid-twentieth century, so-called pop wines have been introduced. Made from such fruits as apples and plums, they are bubbly and inexpensive; but they are not really new. In fact, no new alcoholic beverages have been invented since the eighteenth century.

3

THE USE AND ABUSE
OF ALCOHOL

> Let him either drink or begone.—Cicero, 45 B.C.

> The rule is, don't give in until the wine gives out.—Euripedes, c. 440 B.C.

THE USE OF ALCOHOL

In ancient times, some peoples used beer or wine primarily for religious purposes. The ancient Egyptians believed that knowledge of how to brew beer was a divine gift from their goddess of nature, Isis. Any ceremony honoring her included beer. In Hebrew tradition, wine drinking began with Noah, and wine was important in various religious ceremonies. The Hebrews drank wine every week on the night before the Sabbath. Passover, the most important Jewish holiday, begins with a meal called the Seder, at which wine is served. Jesus and his disciples were celebrating Passover at the Last Supper. Jesus blessed the bread and wine and gave it to his disciples, asking them to continue the practice in his memory. The drinking of wine became an important part of the Christian Communion service. Later, in the Middle Ages, Christian monks tended vineyards and made wines because they felt it was part of their religious duties to do so.

In the Americas, the Aztecs used wine in their religious ceremonies; and the Greeks and Romans honored their respective gods of wine by consuming it in large quantities on their annual feast days.

Among many peoples, including the Greeks and Romans, wine or beer was also served at secular feasts and celebrations, as well as at religious ceremonies. The early Anglo-Saxons drank beer, or ale, to celebrate weddings, to mark the entrance of a young apprentice into a new trade, and at all festivals. When tenant farmers brought the required one-tenth of their crop to their landlords, the landlords rewarded them with ale. The Aztecs made beer from corn and drank it on special occasions.

In Europe, after the discovery of distilled liquor, the idea quickly became widespread that liquor could cure and prevent disease. For many people, drinking began first thing in the morning and was likely to continue at various periods throughout the day.

The Europeans who settled in North America brought their drinking customs with them, of course. In fact, the primary reason why the Pilgrims on the Mayflower decided to land at Plymouth Rock, instead of searching the coast for a better area in which to settle, was that they were low on supplies, "especially beer." The Dutch settlers were no different. In 1660, the town of New Amsterdam in the colony of New Netherlands, later to become New York, had more taverns than any other type of business. In colonial America the general belief was that a man could not do a hard day's work without stopping for a drink now and then. Employers supplied rum to their workers and gave them a break from work about 11 A.M. Shopkeepers kept liquor on hand for their favorite customers. Visiting from house to house always involved drinking, as did all community activities.

Even the church encouraged drinking. In colonial times,

Sunday church services lasted practically all day. The churches were not heated, and in the winter it could become very uncomfortable for the congregation. Thus, taverns were built alongside churches, and the worshippers could go next door to warm themselves with hot toddies, during breaks in the sermon.

Alcohol was an important part of the social and economic life of early America, and it would have been difficult for many Americans to go about their daily activities without it.

During the 1800s, widespread use of alcohol continued, and drinking took on a romantic new image as an essential part of Western life. As the Western frontier era movies show, even the most makeshift boomtown had its saloons, and many aspects of Western life seemed to revolve around them. As one veteran of the 1849 gold rush put it, "You can't do anything in this country without settin' 'em up first."

The same sentiment could easily be expressed today, for liquor pervades in twentieth-century American life. Except in those areas where local laws prohibit the sale of liquor, most restaurants could not stay open if they did not have a liquor license. Bars abound, and it is the custom of many blue-collar workers to go to a bar after work for a few beers before going home. White-collar workers are more likely to do their work-day-associated drinking during long business lunches. Parties are rarely successful without plenty of liquor, and this is true whether the party is in the home, at the office, or in a public building.

Advertising has helped to establish certain American drinking customs. Beer companies sponsor televised sports events, and the image of a man going to the refrigerator for another beer during a break in the Sunday afternoon televised football game is a familiar one. Advertisements also lead us to believe that a fishing trip is not complete without a couple of six-packs of beer, that a really elegant picnic always includes bread and cheese and wine, that a romantic situation requires wine, a cocktail, or a snifter of brandy. In movies, it sometimes seems that people cannot end an evening together without a night-cap. In real life, many individuals have a drink, or two, or three at home after work.

Many schools offer courses in bartending. Some of the students want to learn in order to earn extra money actually tending bar, but some simply want to become expert in mixing drinks. Knowledge of mixing drinks is an important social asset. Gourmet cooking has become more popular in the United States, and French cooking in particular calls for the use of wine, vermouth, or cognac in preparing dishes. It would be unthinkable to serve a gourmet meal without wine, and the custom of drinking wine with meals is on the increase. Domestic wine production is a fast-growing industry, and advertising equates drinking California or New York wines with patriotism. Books on wine selection and appreciation are finding a wide market. Popular songs are filled with references to alcohol, or take alcohol as their subjects. Jingles from beer ads are as familiar to us as the national anthem. It has been estimated that approximately 100 million Americans drink, and there is little reason to expect that this number will not increase.

ALCOHOL ABUSE

> Nobody should drink, but them that can drink.—James Kelly, 1721

> Drunkenness is nothing but voluntary madness.—Seneca, A.D. 65

Drunkenness probably has been common ever since alcohol was discovered. Certainly it has been common since people began to keep records. There were drunks in Egypt and in ancient Rome and Greece. Ancient Egyptian inscriptions warned against drinking too much beer. In ancient Greece, fines were levied against drunks who created public disturbances, and there were regulations providing for the dilution of wine with water. The Greek city-state of Sparta prided itself in the physical and moral health of its citizens. To teach their children how wrong and shameful overdrinking was, Spartans forced their slaves to get drunk in front of the children.

In the Aztec civilization, drunkenness was forbidden and punishable by death. The *I Ching*, written in China 3,000 years ago, cautions against overdrinking in this way: "There is drinking of wine. . . . But if one wets his head, He loses it, in truth." In addition, the ancient Chinese had laws regulating the production and use of alcohol. The Christian Bible warns against drunkenness.

One of the basic laws of the Muslim religion is that the faithful must drink no alcohol. The prophet Muhammad, who founded the religion in the seventh century, and who wrote its laws in a book called the Koran, preached that alcohol was a tool of the devil, used to divide men. Some scholars believed Muhammad banned alcohol because he once lost a battle when his generals became drunk and were unable to fight. Others believe he simply saw much drunkenness in his society and decided it was a chief cause of the problems of that society. Today, the large number of practicing Muslims in the world still abstain from alcohol, and it is proof of the great faith Muhammad commanded from his followers that he could ban alcohol and be obeyed.

Since the properties of alcohol and the effects of alcohol on the body were not understood until the last century, in earlier times alcohol was frequently associated with circumstances beyond human control. Ancient people thought that supernatural spirits inhabited wine and caused drunkenness. Undoubtedly a similar belief was held by Europeans in the Middle Ages, for the custom of referring to wine as "spirits" dates from that period. Another belief in the Middle Ages was that alcohol somehow attracted the Devil and that, when people drank liquor, the Devil entered their bodies through their mouths. To ward off the Devil, people clinked their goblets or other vessels together before drinking. As we now know, people can get quite drunk without any help from the Devil. Yet people still clink their glasses together when drinking a toast.

Until the 1400s few countries in Europe had laws about drinking, and they were intended to protect drinkers by specifying the quality of liquor that was sold. During the 1400s and 1500s these laws were made stronger and new ones were added. The number of taverns in each town was regulated. Tavern owners had to get liquor licenses from the government and were not supposed to serve liquor except to travelers, guests, and working men at the dinner hour. Despite these laws, drunkenness continued. It reached such an alarming rate that many governments finally realized new laws must be passed against the drinkers themselves.

England was the first country to pass such laws, and it is likely that England had the most serious drinking problems. It had the largest fleet in the world and conducted the most ambitious exploration and trade. Sailors everywhere were well known for their drinking habits, and because there were more English sailors they became the most famous. It is no accident that many of the phrases describing drunkenness come from seamen's language or that so many seagoing songs mention alcohol—the phrase *Three sheets to the wind* and the song refrain "Yo-ho-ho, and a bottle of rum!" to cite just two examples.

Early in the 1600s the English Parliament began to pass laws against drinking too much and against drinking on Sundays. When these laws did not seem to make any difference,

Parliament laid a tax upon ale and beer, the favorite alcoholic beverages in England. That was in 1643. Over the years, as beer and ale drinking continued just as before, the tax was raised again and again. Eventually, ale and beer became too expensive for the average citizen. But even this did not stop the English people from drinking. They simply found a cheaper substitute. During the 1600s, England fought several wars with the Netherlands, where English soldiers discovered gin. Since it was made from grain, it was easy to produce in England, and as there was no tax on gin, it soon replaced ale as the national drink.

Gin is stronger than ale, and England's alcohol problem only worsened. Drinking increased so much that England became known as a "nation of drunkards." Parliament passed many laws against gin selling and gin drinking, but it was not until the 1830s that ale became once again the most popular alcoholic beverage in England.

Just as the drinking habit was brought to North America with English and other European colonists, so did drunkenness cross the Atlantic with them. In the colonies, laws regulating drinking were not as strict as they were back in Europe. Too many other problems faced the colonial governments, which were trying to maintain order and bring civilization to the new land. But there were exceptions. Here and there a leader turned his attention to the problem of drinking and tried to do something about it.

One early American who did so was James Oglethorpe, who founded the colony of Georgia in 1733. All new settlers were given forty-four gallons of beer and asked not to drink anything stronger. At the same time, however, they were each given sixty-five gallons of molasses, which they used not for cooking but to make rum.

By the end of the colony's first year, nearly every settler was ailing in some way. It is likely that the colonists were suffering chiefly from the effects of the climate and the rough conditions of a new colony. But Oglethorpe decided rum was the culprit. Afraid that rum would ruin his young colony, Oglethorpe asked the English Parliament to ban rum and brandy.

The new law was a mistake from the start, for the settlers spent most of their time finding ways to get the forbidden liquor. They smuggled it in from South Carolina or made it themselves out of molasses. And when they got it, they drank it faster and got drunker than they had when it was legal. The colony grew very slowly until finally, in 1742, the law was taken off the books. With rum and brandy plentiful again, and the settlers free from worrying about where their next drink was coming from, the colony began to progress once more.

During the 1800s, major changes occurred in American life. Beginning with Eli Whitney's cotton gin, machines that could produce goods faster than humans started being made. Factories sprang up, towns formed around them, and many people, especially the young, left their farms to work in the factories. The nation became industrialized. While drunkenness had been something of a problem in earlier American history, it became a much more serious one after industrialization.

Drunkenness on a small family farm or in a small shop is one thing. Drunkenness in a factory is quite another. One person not doing the job or doing it improperly can affect all the other workers. Production slows down, or too many products are poorly made. Workers getting drunk and not reporting to work put extra work on the other employees. After awhile, those with good attendance records resent the extra work and slow down in their jobs, too.

Drunkenness not only became more of a problem after industrialization, it also increased. Factory jobs did not give people as much satisfaction as working on a farm or in a small shop had done. Small farmers usually owned their own land,

and thus they were working for themselves. Craftspeople, too, often worked for themselves. Even if they worked for others, they had the satisfaction of making a product from beginning to end. A gunsmith would make each individual part of the gun, from wooden handle to smooth metal barrel, fitting all the parts together himself; and when he finished he had an object in which he could take pride.

A worker in a gun factory could not have that satisfaction. He made only one part of the gun. Sometimes he only ran a machine that made the one part. Thus he did not feel much pride in the finished product, because he was separated from it by countless other people and machines. Gun factories could turn out hundreds of guns a day, but the price paid for industrialization was the loss of worker contentment. Working long hours in factories, living in dingy factory towns, many workers turned to liquor for escape. They lost their jobs in the factories. Some took to begging in the streets and wound up in poorhouses. Others turned to crime and were put into jail. Before long the problem of drunkenness in America caused some people to begin a movement to curb the nation's drinking habits, which eventually led to the banning of liquor altogether.

Obviously, alcoholism is not a problem unique to the twentieth century. Nevertheless, it is a serious twentieth-century problem. Of the estimated 100 million people who drink in the United States, approximately one-tenth, or 10 million, are problem drinkers. Since we do not have statistics from earlier centuries with which to compare our present statistics on problem drinking, there is no real proof that alcoholism among adults is more serious today than it was in earlier times. Yet, in all likelihood, the problem *is* more serious today, and the percentage of people who drink excessively is greater than it was in past centuries. The primary reason for this lies in the growth of technology and its effects on human beings.

Consider the inventions and events that have occurred in little more than half a century. Americans have been through two world wars and a variety of conflicts on a less global scale. We have seen the development of the hydrogen and atomic bombs. We have witnessed the destructive capacity of the atomic bomb, and we have read graphic accounts of what a hydrogen bomb can do. We have experienced a fear that no other people in history have known—the fear that our entire country can be destroyed by an enemy, that the entire world could be destroyed should a third world war ever occur. We are familiar with air raids, fallout shelters, and conelrad signals. We realize that our nation has weapons, rockets, and bombs sufficient to destroy the world four times over, and yet we continue to develop new weapons, for we know that other countries are prepared to cause equal destruction.

Within the past seventy-five years we have seen the development of electricity, the telephone, and television; radio, movies, and microwave ovens; photocopiers, computers, and pocket calculators; the automobile, the submarine, and supersonic transport; laser beams, microscopic surgery, and sonar; electric typewriters, vacuum cleaners, and dishwashers; shortwave radios, teletype machines, and satellites. We have sent men to the moon.

Our world has narrowed. There is almost no place on earth we cannot go, if we can afford the plane fare. Even if we choose not to go to Tanganyika or Australia, we can learn about them through television and movies. Through the media, we have experienced every possible human disaster, from earthquakes to floods, to war, to assassinations. We have seen so much misery that we have become desensitized to it. We can talk about an earthquake that kills 18,000 people in Guatemala in the same tone of voice in which we talk about tomorrow's weather.

We have been educated to cynicism. We are constantly informed by the news media how corrupt are our corporations, our politicians, our governmental agencies, our churches, even our media. We do not trust any of them.

Nor do we trust each other. We are increasingly urbanized, increasingly mobile. Some of us encounter more people in one week than our colonial ancestors encountered in their entire lives. No longer do we have deep and permanent roots in one place. We move frequently, our ties with our families are not as strong.

We have more money than any other people in the world. Certainly, we have more money than did people in earlier times, but at the same time television shows us how much money we do not have compared to those who have more. We spend a great deal of time worrying about this and trying to figure out how to get as much money as others have.

And today we have the time to do this worrying. In fact, we have more leisure time than people ever had before in history. But we do not spend this leisure time doing leisurely things. Mostly, we spend it worrying, thinking about ourselves, and trying to figure out how to "be somebody" in an overpopulated world. Thanks to radio and television, newspapers and magazines, movies and books, we have the feeling that everything that ever could be done has already been done by somebody else, that every original idea has already been thought of. There is little left for us to do of which we can be proud. We suffer from the same lack of involvement with what we produce that afflicted the first factory workers, only more so. We do not work in order to take pride in what we produce. Instead, we work to make money to buy the things that will make us proud, knowing all the while that the next day on television we will see someone with five times the things we have.

Things change so quickly today that it is hard to keep up. Alvin Toffler wrote a book about this effect on us, calling it

Future Shock. We have many such labels to apply to our feelings. Psychology has become one of the most popular subjects of twentieth-century thought and conversation; we have the leisure time to think in depth about ourselves and the money to pay a burgeoning number of psychiatrists, psychotherapists, and analysts to help us explore ourselves. Even if we do not seek out professionals, we have read enough and heard enough to use, often incorrectly, such words and phrases as neurotic, paranoid, defensive, schizophrenic, identity crisis, male menopause, approach-avoidance syndrome, diffuse anxiety, and conversion reaction to define the behavior and feelings we and our acquaintances experience. Putting labels on these things is one way in which we cope with living in twentieth-century America.

Some experts on why people drink believe that drinking is another way in which we cope. Other experts disagree and contend that drinking is a means of escape from problems. Both groups are correct in the majority of cases, for escaping is a major means of coping. But identifying behavior by slapping on labels tends to cloud the meaning of that behavior. In many cases, drinking relieves a person's anxiety and thus represents not only an escape from anxiety but also a coping with the anxiety-producing situation.

Excessive drinking, on the other hand, does not represent coping. A situation that drives one to drunkenness remains unchanged or becomes worse when the drinker sobers up. Nor does excessive drinking represent escape from anxiety for any length of time. When sobriety returns, the anxiety comes back, and can be even worse.

Half of all the deaths caused by automobile accidents can be traced to alcohol abuse. Half of all the murders and a quarter of all the suicides that occur in the United States are directly related to alcohol. So are a large proportion of accidents inside and outside the home. Many cases of child abuse occur when a parent is drunk. Family fights and divorces often can be traced to excessive drinking. Just as in the 1800s, alcohol accounts for a large proportion of job absences, for a great deal of crime, for much of the begging in the streets, for a tragic number of wrecked lives. More than in the 1800s or any other period in history, alcoholism is a societal rather than an individual problem. Though we may be more alienated from one another, more a nation of strangers than we were in earlier times, we are at the same time more interdependent. Just at the time when our highly mechanized society is causing more problem drinking, it is demanding more individual mental and physical control. Compare the destructive capacity of an eighteenth-century farmer driving a horse-drawn wagon along a dirt road to a twentieth-century factory worker driving a car on the freeway. Consider an alcoholic bus driver or train engineer. And what about the alcoholic pilot, air traffic controller, or space engineer?

Alcoholism may not be unique to the twentieth century, but in the twentieth century it is uniquely serious. We really do have a problem.

TELLING IT LIKE IT IS

> His eyes were set at eight i' the morning.—Shakespeare, 1599

> Getting pie-eyed. Sozzled. Fried. Plastered. Ossified. Oh, hell. Drunk.—P. G. Wodehouse

An interesting sidelight to alcohol abuse in history is the way people have chosen to describe it. Humans always have believed that words have a kind of magical power. Current examples include the psychological terms mentioned earlier. The feeling is that if one can place a label on human behavior, one does not have to deal with it further, that in defining it one has also understood it. Words are also used to change other people's opinions of things. The Vietnam War produced the word *pacification*. U.S. military operations in Vietnamese villages, which involved mass arrests, imprisonment, even destruction of the villages, were described not as what they were but as pacification, or peace-producing operations. The growing number of aging persons in the United States, and their increased militancy, has led to a change in the terms used to describe them. No longer are they referred to as "old people." "Senior Citizen" was coined to foster a more sympathetic attitude toward the elderly.

Alcohol and drinking have produced not just a few alternative terms but practically an entirely new language. In fact, there are probably more slang terms to describe drinking than there are to describe sex. Ever since it was possible to drink, and to get drunk, people have found interesting ways to describe the condition. As far back as 1000 B.C., the *I Ching* reveals, the Chinese were describing drunkenness as "wetting one's head." In Greece in 200 B.C. a favorite expression was "soaked," and someone really drunk was described as "soaking soaked."

Benjamin Franklin noted the large number of expressions associated with drinking in his day, and being a man of encyclopedic energies as well as interests, he set about compiling a list of them. He published this list in his *Pennsylvania Gazette* in 1733, the same year in which James Oglethorpe was handing out forty-four gallons of beer to each of his colonists and hoping that was all they would drink. Franklin had come up with some 230 words and phrases. He had also noted that the majority of words and phrases *meant* but did not actually *say* "drunk." "It argues some Shame in the Drunkards themselves," he commented, "in that they have invented number-less Words and Phrases to cover their folly."

Things have not changed since Ben Franklin's time. While many of the words and phrases on his list are no longer in use today, some are still familiar: boozy, in the cups, cockeyed, intoxicated, juicy (today we say juiced), mellow, oiled, stiff, stewed, tipsy. And, of course, many new ones have been added to replace the old. Today we all are familiar with such words and phrases as looped, under the table, fried, plowed, pie-eyed, zonked, soused, flattened, and plastered, and new expressions are introduced all the time. The reasons are the same as they were in the 1700s. Drunkenness is embarrassing, and we usually find other words and other ways to talk about things that embarrass us.

Still, a change in term does not guarantee a change in attitude, or at least not forever. It took fifty years for the term *alcoholic* to come into general use in place of the word *drunkard*. The introduction of the term *alcoholic* was supposed to create more sympathy for people with serious drinking problems. But, nowadays, *alcoholic* is just one step above *drunkard* in social acceptance. Both terms imply the dregs (note associations with alcohol) of society. It is interesting to listen to the way people refer to drinking, especially excessive drinking, and to note how rarely anyone utters the word *drunk*.

4

YOUNG PEOPLE
AND PROBLEM DRINKING

> Wine is the first weapon the devils use in attacking the young.—St. Jerome, c. 420

> If you cannot carry your liquor when you are young, boy, you will be a water-carrier when you are old.—Anacharsis, c. 590 B.C.

THE HISTORY OF YOUTHFUL ALCOHOLISM

Just because we are experiencing the first *widespread* use of alcohol by young persons, this is not to say that problem drinking among youth did not exist in earlier times. Disturbed by excessive drinking in ancient Athens, Greek philosopher Plato recommended stricter regulations than were in force at that time. One of these regulations would prohibit all drinking by boat pilots, slaves, pregnant women, and *persons under eighteen.*

Throughout history and in practically every society there have been homeless youths, living on the streets or along the roads; living by their wits, stealing, begging. They have followed older vagabonds and imitated their rough talk, their smoking, and their drinking.

Their numbers have depended on the conditions of the particular society in which they found themselves. The roads of seventeenth- and eighteenth-century Europe were thronged with bands of rogues and youthful vagabonds, the city streets abounded with pickpockets. Western Europe was overpopulated, and this situation, combined with customs of class and inheritance, led inevitably to a large population of shiftless, rough-living, and frequently drunken youth. They were of the peasant class, primarily the children of poor farm couples who had large families not only to ensure an adequate workforce on the farm but because they knew little or nothing about birth control. Of these children, only the eldest son had any real future to look forward to. He would inherit his parents' property. For the other children, the societally approved choices were dismal: to rent a poor cottage and do paid labor, to work other people's land, or to travel to a large city to find menial work. Many rejected all three and chose instead a life of wandering, which usually led to crime and drunkeness.

The colonization of the New World represented a safety valve for the increased unrest and class tension of overpopulated Europe. The first settlers were primarily of the peasant class, willing to face the rigors of pioneer life, for there was nothing worth remaining for in their homelands. The companies that directed settlement of the new colonies favored families, believing they would be a more stable population than unattached adults or young people. But the harshness of life in the new colonies soon produced a sizable number of orphans.

While the settlements were small, the care of these orphans was taken over rather easily by the community. When they reached their teens, the boys were apprenticed to craftsmen in order to learn a trade, the girls went to live with families as household helpers. This ideal arrangement, in both cases, provided an equal give-and-take in a homelike atmosphere. The young people gave their labor, and in return the craftsmen or housewives saw to their education, their moral upbringing, and their physical needs. Most such arrangements, however, fell far short of the ideal. The youth were often treated like servants, or worse, like slaves. Aware that their work was valued far more than they themselves were, the boys and girls used their work as a weapon. They "accidently" damaged property, they did not do the work assigned to them. More and more they banded together, seeking from each other the warmth and companionship that they did not get in the houses and shops where they lived and worked. They became a separate and alienated underclass. According to a contemporary observer:

> The lads and wenches met when they wished, they drank rum at the taverns and they danced together til late in the night. Reproved, they threatened to burn the town down over the ears of the burghers.

The problem of vagabond youth grew worse during the Revolutionary War, for the cities were in an almost constant state of turmoil. After the war, the departure of the British colonial governments also meant the departure of the old institutions of authority necessary to maintain an ordered society. The new governments and peacekeeping forces took time to organize, and violence involving former apprentices and orphans who had left the towns for the excitement of the cities increased.

During the 1800s, two new factors were introduced, which encouraged wandering youth and drinking problems among youth. The first was industrialization. Many of the factory jobs and machine operations could be handled by children, and young people became an important part of the work force, though the bands of vagabond youth were generally too accustomed to an unstructured life to join the work force for any length of time. Besides, they could make a better living at petty theft. Many children of farm families remained on the farm, but some left the farm early to get jobs and thus be on their own. Restless, they traveled about, prized their independence, and copied the behavior of the adults with whom they came in contact. Industrialization caused an increase in problem drinking among adults; it did the same for youth.

The second factor was immigration. Waves of Europeans, first from Ireland, later from northern and southern Europe, were deposited on the eastern seaboard. As most did not have money to travel further, they settled in the port cities where they landed. These cities already had small ethnic populations, and the new arrivals sought out people of their own kind. They crowded into the ethnic ghettos, which nearly burst from overpopulation. But the newcomers were unwelcome in most of the other neighborhoods in the cities. New York received the greatest influx of immigrants, and before long the overcrowded conditions, the discrimination, and the poverty had made the ethnic neighborhoods notorious for their crime and squalor. The first organized street gangs emerged from these neighborhoods, but unlike street gangs today they were composed of men, not teen-agers. The youth, either orphaned or unwanted, roamed the streets singly or in small groups, scavenging for food or salable items, doing odd jobs, sleeping in cellars and doorways, committing petty crimes. Some were alcoholics. In 1867, in New York City 3,658 boys and girls between the ages of ten and fifteen were arrested for various reasons. One of the boys, a fifteen-year-old, was committed to a state institution as a confirmed drunk, and his thirteen-year-old brother killed himself in a fit of depression.

Some twenty years later, Jacob Riis, whose photographs and writings of "the other half" of society are still the greatest documents of lower-class life of the time, studied the slums of New York and its inhabitants, paying particular attention to the children.

Aware of the problem of drunkenness among the adult population of the slums, he decided to investigate briefly the incidence of drinking among children. He chose at random a saloon in an East Side tenement district and stationed a friend there to count the children who went into the saloon and emerged with beer jugs. Later, he wrote:

> He reported as the result of three and a half hours' watch at noon and in the evening a total of fourteen—ten boys and a girl under ten years of age, and three girls between ten and fourteen years, not counting a little boy who bought a bottle of ginger. It was a cool, damp day; not a thirsty day, or the number would probably have been twice as great. There was not the least concealment about transaction in any of the fourteen cases. The children were evidently old customers.

Riis's investigation was encyclopedic, covering all aspects of tenement life, and thus he was not concerned primarily with alcoholism among either adults or youth. But he did relate statistics on the incidence of alcoholism among parents of children in one reformatory (38.4 percent had drunken parents, and another 13 percent had parents of "doubtful sobriety") and cited some examples of youthful drunkenness.

He related how a fifteen-year-old named Harry Quill disappeared one February, and no one even bothered to look for him. Two months later, his body was found at the bottom of an air shaft. In September, one of his friends confessed to throwing Harry down the shaft. Riis reported:

Harry was drunk, he said, and attacked him on the roof with a knife. In the struggle he threw him into the air shaft. Fifteen years old, and fighting drunk! The mere statement sheds a stronger light on the sources of child vagabondage in our city than I could do, were I to fill the rest of my book with an enumeration of them.

However, it is a good deal oftener the father who gets drunk than the boy. Not all, nor even a majority, of the boys one meets at the lodging-houses are of that stamp.

Nevertheless, youthful alcoholism, no matter how small in percentage in relation to the total population, was considered scandalous by society then, although very little was done about the situation. The main reason was that the youths who were getting drunk were, in the eyes of the society, "bad" to begin with. They were the young hoodlums and street urchins of whom the society expected such behavior.

As a matter of fact, it was generally true that the youthful alcoholics were the children of the poor, orphans without any home or family. Rarely was a drinking problem found within the middle or upper classes. Beginning with Prohibition, the situation changed. During the time alcohol was illegal, it became fashionable for middle- and upper-class youth to drink. After Prohibition was repealed, these youth were less concerned with drinking and it lost its faddish aspects. Yet drinking continued, on a less active basis.

Over the years, drinking became accepted practice among teen-agers, although it was illegal. At colleges, beer was a natural part of parties and other campus activities, and the authorities looked the other way as long as the drinking was confined to the campus. Some high schoolers drank on weekends, but most took their first real drinks on graduation night. Young servicemen rarely had trouble buying a drink, even though they were underage. It seemed to most people that if these young men were old enough to defend their country, they should be allowed to drink.

Meanwhile, changes in the nation's drinking habits made it easier for young people to drink. Fifty years ago, more drinking was done at public drinking places than anywhere else. Today, more drinking is done at social affairs and in the home. And, of course, it is much easier for young people under legal age to drink in these circumstances. Many parents allow, and even encourage, their children to drink in the home before they have reached the legal drinking age. Some of these parents do so because drinking is part of their ethnic tradition. Others do so because they see no harm in it. They do not allow their sons and daughters a highball before dinner, but they enjoy seeing a child drink the foam from a glass of beer or taking a sip from a mixed drink. They associate drinking with adulthood, consider it "cute" and natural that their children wish to imitate the behavior of adults and, when their children reach legal drinking age, generally celebrate the occasion in a fitting manner. Still other parents encourage drinking, under controlled circumstances, by their underage children because they want their children to be accepted by their peers. Parents will purchase liquor for their children's parties, or will make their own liquor available. They feel that they would rather their children drank in the home than outside it.

Teen-age drinking increased markedly during the 1960s, but few really noticed it, probably because teen-age use of illegal drugs also reached a high point during that decade. Parents who realized their teen-agers were drinking were not alarmed. In fact, they were relieved that their sons and daughters were not on drugs. The police reacted in much the same manner. They were looking for drugs, not booze. They wanted to arrest dope pushers, not people who were buying beer for underage kids. Meanwhile, the pressures and desires that were causing kids to turn to drugs were also causing them to turn to alcohol. And since no one seemed to worry much about youthful drinkers, more and more became addicted to the drug alcohol. By the early 1970s, teen-age alcoholism was a serious problem and society recognized it. But by the time people had thoroughly digested the idea of a teen-age drinking epidemic, studies were beginning to show a sizable number of problem drinkers among adolescents and even younger kids. Nine-year-olds are missing school because they are too hung over to attend. Ten-year-olds are sneaking bottles from their parents' liquor closets. Eleven-year-olds take thermoses of vodka and orange juice or scotch and milk for lunch. Twelve-year-olds are admitted to hospital emergency rooms vomiting blood. Today, there are some 500,000 alcoholics between the ages of ten and nineteen, and it is estimated that one out of every fifteen young people today will eventually become an alcoholic. Throughout its history, alcohol has contributed to wrecked lives, but today more and more of the lives that are being wrecked are lives that hardly have begun.

WHY YOUNG PEOPLE DRINK

> Wine works the heart up, wakes the wit; There is no cure 'gainst age but it.—John Fletcher, c. 1616

> The flowing bowl—whom has it not made eloquent? Whom has it not made free, even amid pinching poverty?—Horace, 20 B.C.

There are many reasons why young people drink, just as there are many reasons why adults drink. In attempting to explain the basis of youthful drinking, psychologists and others have pointed to many of the conditions of twentieth-century life mentioned in the previous chapter: the awareness of the possibility of worldwide destruction, the alienation, the utter breakneck *speed* of life. Certainly these conditions affect young people. Some young people are even able to explain their drinking by citing these factors, but when they do they are really avoiding more basic reasons. As a general rule, it takes several more years of experience than the average adolescent or teen-ager has lived to be able to understand the conditions of society that affect him or her. As a matter of fact, the majority of adults never understand themselves how their lives are affected by the larger society, which is why they tend to rely on psychologists and philosophers and social thinkers to tell them how they are affected.

When asked why they drink, most young people give simple and direct answers. With minor variations here and there, they are the same reasons why adults drink. The fact that they do not mention the atomic bomb or the effects of television violence does not mean these factors do not affect them profoundly. It is simply that the conditions of their own lives affect them more directly. Four answers are given most frequently by young people who are questioned as to why they drink. In order of importance, they are: because of parental and societal influences, because it makes them feel good, because their friends drink, because they have serious emotional problems.

PARENTAL AND SOCIETAL INFLUENCES

We have already discussed the societal influences on drinking. Alcohol is all around us. In fact, it is intricately connected with our society's attitudes about sociability. The hospitable host will generally greet visitors with "What can I get you to drink?" We may not have a god of wine and a feast day on which we honor him, as had the ancient Greeks and Romans, but our New Year's Eve celebrations are comparable to the feast of Bacchus. Alcohol, or drinking, is also involved in our definition of adulthood. As a general rule, the legal drinking age has also been the age of majority, twenty-one years old in the past, now more often eighteen years old since eighteen-year-olds have the franchise.

Advertising equates drinking with "the good life," with romance, with virile men. Since the so-called pop fruit wines have been introduced, the marketers of those wines have aimed their advertising campaigns at young adults. According to the ads, these wines are the "in" beverage for young people, and the ads have been very successful in selling their product to the target audience. Sales of strawberry, apple, and other fruit wines have increased ten times in the past four years, and it is young people who are drinking them. Most adults prefer beer, mixed drinks, highballs, or more traditional wines.

Thus, societal attitudes and customs and the type of advertising society accepts are important influences on young people and on their drinking habits. More important, however, are parental attitudes and drinking habits.

The following statement is characteristic of many middle-class youngsters who drink:

> In my case, my family approved of social drinking and encouraged the drink before dinner, the brandy afterward, the scotch midevening. But there was one rule: I must never get drunk.

A 1972 study of junior high and high school drinking habits in Berkeley, California, revealed that over half the students in each of the grades surveyed were with their parents when they first used alcohol. Other studies show similar results. Here are some typical answers to the question, "When did you first drink alcohol?"

> My aunt gave me my first can of beer when I was about fourteen and that started it.

> My dad is always bitching about my drinking, but strange as it seems, he was the one who got me started—I was fourteen.

> At thirteen I was sent to live with an uncle in Nevada because my stepfather and I just couldn't get along. He felt that if, at an early age, you became aware of your capacity for booze, you wouldn't have any trouble with it later. So I had the freedom to drink anything in the house.

> I started drinking when I was thirteen, the summer before seventh grade. My father drank beer and I wanted to be like him. He would give me tastes of his beer, and I developed a craving for it.

It is not surprising that parents offer their teen-agers a taste of their alcohol, especially beer. Many parents expect their children to be drinking in a few years, anyway. But it seems nearly as acceptable to introduce children to drinking at a much younger age. Many restaurants have fruit drinks called Shirley Temples to serve to children while their parents are having a before-dinner cocktail. Part of the fun of many a New Year's Eve party held in the home is allowing a very young child to stay up until midnight and to taste grown-up drinks. Some young drinkers trace their experience with alcohol back to age seven, or younger:

The first time I got drunk I was four or five years old. My parents had a New Year's Eve party, and I joined the grown-ups. It was memorable, and I didn't get sick at all.

I must have been about five or six. I remember having a tea party for my dolls in the basement of our cellar and inviting my parents. My father had a beer and he let me sip the foam off the top. I loved it, and would always ask for the foam off my parents' beers.

When I was about seven, my dad started letting me have beer whenever I wanted it.

Thus, many parents actively encourage their children to experience liquor, although they generally frown on regular drinking and on drinking outside the home. When they find the level of liquid in their liquor bottles suspiciously lower, or when their teen-ager arrives home with liquor on his or her breath, they may be disturbed. But, rather than punishing their sons and daughters, or taking any serious steps to deal with the drinking behavior, they rationalize away their concern by reminding themselves that "at least they're not on drugs."

My parents don't mind if I drink; they like it better than drugs, anyway.

Most of my friends drink, and most of the parents don't seem to mind. If you smoked dope, they'd mind.

My parents didn't care. They said, "As long as it's legal, that's all we worry about."

Further proof of parental influence on young people's drinking habits can be found in studies that show that young people who drink are much more likely to have parents who drink than parents who do not drink. Young people are not only influenced by what their parents do but also by what their parents say. Among young people whose parents suggest they do not drink, four out of ten will follow their advice. Youths whose parents do not counsel them about alcohol are twice as likely to drink, for eight out of ten of them do. This is not to say that parents who drink automatically influence their children to become problem drinkers. But it is natural for children to imitate their parents. Parents are adults, and what they do represents adult behavior. Kids want to be grown up, and the most logical and accessible role models are their parents. We tend to believe adolescents and teen-agers are most influenced by others of their own age, and in some areas they are. But in the case of drinking, though the influence of the peer group is important, parents have the greatest influence.

DRINKING TO FEEL GOOD, OR BETTER

One undeniable advantage in drinking is that in moderate quantities it has a very relaxing effect. And, because alcohol removes some of the inhibitions, it can cause a person to become more talkative, less tense in social situations, and generally to feel good. This effect is important to anyone who drinks, no matter what age he or she is, but young people who drink often place a particularly strong emphasis on it.

Drinking makes me feel happy and helps me have a good time.

There isn't much to do around here on weekends, so a bunch of us usually get some six-packs and go to a place on the outskirts of town. We get high and race our cars.

The adolescent and teen-age years are a time of awakening individuality. While home and family remain the center of most teen-agers' lives, they are increasingly conscious of the outside world and of the possibilities available to them. They begin to see themselves as separate entities and, in fact, go through a period of wishing not to be seen with their parents and feeling acutely uncomfortable with adult acquaintances when not in structured situations such as school. At the same time, the awareness of individuality is not so strong that the adolescent or teen-ager does not need a great deal of support and reinforcement. This is where the peer group comes in. More than anything else, young persons want to be part of a group, to be like others of the same age. They want to wear the same clothes, engage in the same activities, experience the same things. It is very important to be assured their friends are feeling what they are feeling, for the adolescent and teen-age years can be frightening and lonely.

Physical alterations are occurring in the body. New emotions are experienced, such as the first romantic interest in the opposite sex, and the first real depression. Emotional ups and downs are drastic and seemingly uncontrollable. During these years, young people become acutely aware of themselves. They spend a great deal of time being concerned about their physical appearance. They are growing, but their various body parts do not develop at the same rate. His ears may suddenly seem much too big in proportion to his head. Her legs seem to lengthen a foot while her torso does not grow at all. Hormonal changes can cause self-consciousness—and not only from those changes that affect the sexual organs. She gets a bad case of acne. His voice begins to crack. They can no longer be certain that their bodies will follow the commands of their brains—perfectly logical commands that their bodies never had trouble with before.

There is a feeling of living inside an alien body and being at the mercy of strange emotional urges. Young people spend a lot of time looking at and thinking about themselves. Who is he or she? How does he or she exist in relation to parents, friends, the universe. Teen-agers have conflicting feelings about the adult world. They see much in it that they do not like; yet they know that in a few short years they will be part of it. They realize they will leave home, begin a career, perhaps take a mate. It is frightening to think about. At the same time they yearn for the freedom and power that they associate with adulthood.

They tend to "let it all hang out." They have not yet learned to cope with their insecurities. In later years, they will learn to hide their feelings better, to build up defenses that most people will not be able to see through. But for now, their defenses are practically transparent, and their social awkwardness is very conspicuous.

Many young people drink to hide their insecurities and their social awkwardness. The fellow who is shy around girls suddenly finds that he can talk to them easily after he's had a couple of drinks. The girl who feels unattractive ceases to worry about her appearance when she is high and finds she can join in the activities of her group wholeheartedly. It is true that alcohol acts to inhibit certain brain impulses and thus causes the drinker to have fewer inhibitions. But in these cases the effects of alcohol are more *psychological* than physical. The alcohol itself does not put the drinker on top of a situation; the drinker expects the alcohol to do so and thus feels that it has. Social awkwardness can be overcome without any help from alcohol, but many young people take a shortcut, substituting alcohol for thought and inner personality development.

The trouble is, the shortcut is really not a shortcut at all. Rather, it is more like a detour. Alcohol is an artificial means of overcoming insecurity in social situations. Once it is removed, it leaves no residual effect. The shy person who cannot seem to carry on a conversation without having a few drinks does not learn how to carry on a conversation in a nondrinking situation. While drinking may be a means of social advancement in the short run, in the long run it is the surest instrument of social retardation. In other words, whatever chronological age the young person is when he or she starts relying on the psychological effects of alcohol, that is the social age he or she will be when the problem drinking stops. A boy or girl who starts drinking at age fourteen and stops at age eighteen, is not likely to be a normally mature eighteen-year-old. He or she will look eighteen, but socially will function more like a fourteen-year-old. Needless to say, the social problems encountered at age eighteen are generally more demanding than those experienced at age fourteen. Rather than solving anything, alcohol only makes the situation worse.

Many young users of alcohol insist they do not drink becaused they have social problems; rather, they simply enjoy the kick it gives them. Some may be covering up, unwilling to admit feelings of shyness or awkwardness. But it is reasonable to assume that others are telling the truth. They are not suffering from *personal* problems but are responding instead to a general social problem that afflicts a majority of young people and thus the whole society. It is the feeling of boredom and apathy and lack of direction that seems to have been spawned after World War II and to have come to maturity in the 1970s, following very closely the development of a large middle-class population.

In the United States, the war had the greatest impact on young adults. Young men fought the war; young women worked in the war industries and waited for the men to come home. After the Allies won, the men returned heady with victory, for in that war it was considered patriotic and courageous to fight. The enemy was clearly an enemy not only to the

United States but to humankind as a whole. The rest of the country shared this victorious feeling. War had caused the nation to prosper, and the country was proud of its prosperity and proud of its young fighting men. As a reward, they were given the most liberal educational benefits in history and the men, who had grown up during the depression, saw education as the best way to get ahead in the world and to get the material things of which their parents had been deprived. Thousands enrolled in college, their education financed by the G.I. Bill.

The end of the war also ushered in a new emphasis on family life. The men were back home now, their future assured through education and the general economic prosperity. The postwar "baby boom" occurred, and with the sudden increase in the infant population came a new concern for children. The United States became a child-oriented society. The parents of these postwar babies wanted their children's lives to be different from their own early years. They wanted to give them the things they could not have—material things like toys and clothes, emotional things like a carefree childhood and a secure future. Americans became even more future-oriented, investing their own hopes and dreams in their children.

But, while on the surface the childhood of those who grew up in the fifties and early sixties was carefree and comfortable, beneath the surface these children were being affected by events outside their homes, over which their parents had little control. The Cold War began in the 1950s. Here and there, as in Korea, there were minor "hot" wars, but, in general, an uneasy peace settled over the world. An ideological struggle began between the Communist nations and the nations of the so-called Free World. The atomic bomb had been dropped at Hiroshima and Nagasaki—and the hydrogen bomb was being developed. Nations were amassing stockpiles of new and devastating weapons. What if a nation decided to use them?

Air raid drills became a common and frightening experience for grade school children. Families built bomb shelters and stocked them with food and oxygen. Television, a new form of entertainment in many homes in the early and mid-1950s, could become a strange and alien object when the screen suddenly showed a black-and-white bull's-eye image and a solemn voice announced, "This is a test." No matter how reassuring their parents, how numerous their toys, how often they were told their future held bright and endless possibilities, the youngsters growing up during these years could not help but feel an intense and nameless fear.

By the time they entered college (and by the early 1960s it was almost as expected that middle-class children go to college as it was for them to go to high school), these products of the postwar baby boom were the most aware, educated, and pampered group of young people in United States history. Through television, they had been made aware of the outside world more than any previous generation had, and through developments in aviation there were few corners of that outside world that were not directly accessible. Because of the Cold War and the threat of greater technological advancements by Communist countries, they were also more highly educated in math and science than previous generations. Because of their doting parents and because, due to their going to college, their true confrontation with the outside world (being on their own, having to work to totally support themselves) would be delayed another four years at least, they were more pampered than any previous generations had been.

Given all this, it came as a shock to much of adult society when the collegians of the sixties, many of them anyway, started to make trouble. Television and expanded communications in general had taught them that there were few absolutes. Morals, customs, ways of thinking were not grouped around opposite poles of right or wrong. Rather, they were based on time, place, experience, culture, and a number of other variables. Ideas and actions could be wrong and right at the same time. These youngsters' higher educations had emphasized the qualities that our society believed would keep the United States technologically ahead of its competitors: independence of thought, ability to make decisions, inventiveness, willingness to challenge tradition. Institutions of higher education stressed these qualities even more strongly and offered a much freer environment in which they could develop. Students began returning home during vacations with ideas their parents considered radical.

A considerable number of college-age people were asking questions that their parents, if they had once asked the same questions silently, certainly never would have uttered publicly. They were questions about morality, about racial equality, about economic opportunity, about the importance of religion, about politics, about materialism. Suddenly, everyone was talking about "the generation gap"; parents and children were looking at each other as if they were from different planets.

Young whites who had enjoyed material comfort and physical security all their lives were spending their summers helping poor, black southerners register to vote, engaging in civil rights marches and sitting in at segregated lunch counters. Children of business executives were dropping out of college and settling in communes in the Southwest. Sons and daughters who had had their first dates at age seventeen and had never sworn before in their lives were demanding co-ed dormitories at college and freedom to use obscene language.

There were two primary focuses for young people during the late 1960s. Both were forms of rebellion. One was active —a demand that the establishment, the way older generations did things, be changed. One was passive—a refusal to deal with the establishment. The active focus was the Vietnam War, the passive focus was the drug scene.

The antiwar movement is sufficiently fresh in everyone's mind not to require elaborate explanation. It was the most intense challenge in United States history to the way government operates and the way wealthy nations deal with poorer nations, particularly the way the United States saw its role in the affairs of the rest of the world. In terms of the generation gap, it probably brought about the widest split, for the young people who were protesting the war in Vietnam were the sons and daughters of a generation that had wholeheartedly supported United States involvement in World War II. The children could not see any similarity in the two war experiences, and the parents could not see any difference.

The widespread use of drugs was another matter. It represented a "turning off" to the establishment rather than an attempt to change it. Neither drugs nor the reasons for using them were new in the United States. Drugs had been brought into the urban ghettos shortly after the end of Prohibition, when the organized underworld, grown powerful and wealthy from bootlegging, had found a new way to maintain their wealth and power by getting a substantial portion of the ghetto population hooked on drugs. What was new was the wide use of drugs among middle-class youth. The pampered, educated middle-class youngsters were feeling the same alienation, or an alienation equal in intensity, to that felt by the poor and socially downtrodden lower class. They were so estranged from their parents that they rejected the most basic beliefs and customs of their parents. Unwilling or unable to substitute adequate new beliefs and customs, they turned to drugs and simply escaped from the conflict altogether. First marijuana, then hard drugs such as cocaine and heroin moved across the boundaries of the ghettos and into the suburbs. And the suburban middle-class kids took up their own psychedelic drugs, such as LSD, as well.

At first, adult society used the same tactic to fight both youth movements. Police were sent to quell antiwar disturbances, just as they were dispatched as troops in the war against drugs. Interestingly, however, at first their targets differed depending on the movement. Young antiwar demonstrators, no matter how wealthy their parents might be, were clubbed and arrested and jailed right along with the others. Young, affluent, middle-class drug users were dismissed with a reprimand, or given fines rather than sentences. It was the drug pushers whom the police were after, not the drug users.

Of course, the antiwar movement was much more visible. If they were to be seen and heard, those against the war had to demonstrate in public. The police did not have to go searching for them. In the eyes of the establishment, the antiwar movement was a visible example of lawlessness, which had to be quickly and violently quelled. On the other hand, the movement to drugs was underground. It attacked societal mores indirectly, not publicly. Also, it was still associated with urban ghettos, not middle-class colleges. The attitude of society was that a minority of middle-class young people were falling prey to unscrupulous pushers, and it was the pushers who were the targets of the police.

As the antiwar movement matured, society began to make adjustments to it. The protest was seen as simply part of an overall rebellion, and many concessions were made in hopes that protest against the war would diminish. College students were given ever-increasing freedoms and rights in academic and extracurricular areas. Still the antiwar protest continued and increased. The major factor in favor of the young protesters was their numbers. They constituted a sizable "political interest" group. Gradually, much of the nation came to agree that United States involvement in the Vietnam War was wrong. Veterans of the antiwar movement would like to think that they succeeded because they had right on their side. However, it is likely that United States withdrawal from the war had more to do with the size of the antiwar movement. If it was not large enough to bring about an end to United States involvement, it was certainly large enough to prevent deeper involvement. The section of the population that simply grew tired of the stalemate situation in Southeast Asia, combined with the people who were deeply against the war, were enough to bring about the end of the war.

The establishment fared better in the war on drugs. When the drug scene emerged from underground and became quite evident among the college youth across the nation, it ceased to be an individual or family problem and became a national problem. Emphasis had previously been on catching the pushers; after a time, the target population was enlarged to include the users. Sons and daughters of famous and prominent people were arrested for drug possession, and in many states drug abuse laws were enacted that provided for stricter enforcement. A federal crackdown on importation of drugs caused scarcities in the drug market, and new drug substitutes like methadone were developed. The drug movement lost strength. For many young people, drugs were just too expensive and too risky. Those who could not kick the habit had to spend double the time and money feeding it. The drug movement did not vanish, but, essentially, it did go underground again.

Meanwhile, the adolescent younger brothers and sisters of the college age young people of the sixties watched and listened and learned. In some areas, especially in the cities and near college campuses, they formed minimovements of their own. They, too, were against the war. They also experimented with drugs. They dressed in Army surplus garb and let their hair grow long. They demonstrated for an end to high school dress codes and for increased student rights. They yearned to be old enough to have more freedom to rebel, whether actively by joining the antiwar movement or passively by joining the drug culture.

However, these younger brothers and sisters were born too late. By the time they reached college age the pullout of United States troops from Southeast Asia had already begun. Drug use was still rampant, but soon the campaign against users would begin. The entire active youth movement had diminished considerably. For those involved in the antiwar movement at its height, the end to United States involvement in Vietnam came too late. They had so exhausted themselves that they had little energy to counsel younger reinforcements in the fight against the establishment. For awhile afterward, the momentum of the battle against the war continued, bringing about the lowering of the voting age to eighteen and more student rights and freedoms on both the high school and college levels. But apathy and cynicism were setting in. There emerged a widespread feeling that the individual was powerless in the face of the military-industrial-political complex and that as a result of the experience with the antiwar movement, this complex had learned how to keep disgruntled individuals from uniting. In the early 1970s, most of the sixties activists gave up the fight, and those who were just coming of age in the seventies realized it was useless to get into it in the first place. College campuses were peaceful once again, and in many high schools the students gave the fight for their rights over to legislators courting the eighteen-year-old vote.

In a way, the entire country was exhausted. The Vietnam War and the protest against it took a lot out of everyone, as did the civil rights struggles of the 1960s. The entire decade seemed to have been one of social unrest and violence. The world had become terribly complicated and difficult to cope with. People old enough to remember began to speak of "the good old days," and the way they described them made them sound very attractive to those not old enough to remember.

A wave of nostalgia swept the country. Movies depicting life in earlier decades became box-office hits, *American Graffiti*, *The Day of the Locust*, *The Great Gatsby*, to name a few. Television situation comedies soon followed suit with "Happy Days," as did the detective dramas such as "Ellery Queen" and "Baretta." Television also served as the forum for advertisements of nostalgia records, "The Greatest Hits of the 40s," "The Greatest Hits of the 50s," and so on. Fashion designers reintroduced old styles; even dancing returned to a previous era with the Hustle. College curricula offered courses on the thirties and the twenties, and students whose older siblings had engaged in boycotts engaged instead in panty raids. The Great Depression of the 1930s took on a romantic quality and, almost as if in response, the United States began to sink into a 1970s version of it.

Adolescents and teen-agers today are a product of all the foregoing. More than anything else, perhaps, they feel they are living in the wrong time. They missed the exciting activism and the political idealism of the 1960s. They missed the supposedly wonderful decades as depicted by the nostalgia movement. The 1970s depression is not nearly as romantic as they think the 1930s Great Depression must have been. They find themselves pressured to go to college or get a job, when the headlines in every morning's newspaper tell them unemployment is rampant in all sectors of the economy. They are expected to marry and have children when they are bombarded with divorce and overpopulation statistics. They do dances and wear clothing similar in style to those of the 1940s, all the while knowing that their 1940s counterparts had never heard of the energy crisis or of environmental pollution. They are a part of the present generation, which is aware of the possibility that there may be no future, not only for them but for anyone.

They have a lot of time to think about such things. Middle-class adults have more leisure time than ever, and their children have an even greater amount. Except for going to school, there is really nothing to do. Their chores, if they have any, are minimal. Their homework, unless they go to a tough school, takes about an hour per night. Their parents give them things, and in return they often resent their parents. The generation gap continues. Now, more than ever before, young people see their parents as leading dead-end lives, fighting and divorcing, worrying over money, constantly concerned with material possessions, and caught up in a syndrome in which they have no control over their existence. They either reject such a life-style altogether, or cynically resign themselves to it as the way things are. In either case, they are not happy about it. And increasingly, unhappy young people are turning to alcohol.

Now that drugs are so expensive and hard to get and now that drug use carries such severe penalties, drinking seems the easiest way for many young people to escape the boring realities of life without taking serious risks with the law. Liquor, after all, is legal, and in many states the legal drinking age is now eighteen. Adults are still so concerned about drugs that a drinking problem seems to them minor in comparison. Certainly, drinking does not appear to be a very serious rebellion against parents (after all, they drink, too), but young people do not see much point in rebelling anyway. They worry about ending up essentially as their parents have. They dream about pioneering in the wilderness, of loving but not necessarily marrying. But they know that is in the future, and that the future is a long way off. In the meantime, they drink.

PEER GROUP PRESSURE

In a group, there are two factors that lead to power. One is to be stronger than any of the others in the group, and the other is to belong to the majority. A study of adolescent and teen-age groups can lead to an understanding of almost all groups. Who decides to make up a special code language? Who first wears a distinctive hat or shirt? Who talks while most everyone else listens? Who is more sure of him- or herself? Do the majority do such and such or not? The influence of the group is strong, no matter what the age range; however, the peer group is particularly important for the adolescent or teen-ager who wants to break away from the family but at the same time quite naturally needs an "alternate family" for support and reinforcement.

During the teen-age and adolescent years, one's friends become very important and the following statements are two of the most frequently given reasons why a youngster starts drinking:

"All my friends drink."

"I didn't want to look square, so I started drinking."

At home a teen-ager may be crying, "I want to be an individual," while at school or with friends he or she may have just the opposite desire. Individuality is actually frowned upon by the youthful peer group, although the group is unlikely to recognize differentness from the rest of the group as individuality. Actually, the youthful group does not establish its identity by what it *is* as much as by what it *is not*. Among the things considered "out of it" by the average youthful peer group are studying too hard (making good grades is okay as long as you appear to do it without any effort); wearing white socks with dark leather shoes; having to be in at ten o'clock when everyone else can stay out until eleven; not being interested in girls, if you are male, or boys, if you are female (you must be gay!); coming to school too dressed up; being too shy; being "too nice" (not engaging in the same kind of sexual experimentation as others your age); being fat; being too dumb (studying, but still flunking); being poor; flaunting your parents' wealth; not knowing the latest slang words; not being able to dance. The list could go on and on. Adult groups are not *quite* as rigid but they do exert similar pressure to conform in their attitudes toward drinking.

Because so many adults do drink, at least on social occasions, the nondrinking adult is almost automatically an outsider. This is true of adults who have never been drinkers and even more true of adults who once drank and now are trying to abstain. There is great pressure on them to resume the habit. Increasingly, the nondrinking adolescent or teen-ager feels pressure to conform, to take a drink, to get high at a party where everyone else is drinking. Adults have more experience and greater realization that they can find other groups in which they will be accepted, though they may be hard to find. Adults also are more likely to have a more defined sense of identity and respect for their own individuality. Adolescents and teen-agers need the support of a group, and they haven't the same range of choices that adults have. For a growing number of young people, refusal to take a drink means being placed among the outsiders.

Once, this intense pressure was felt mainly by boys, whose refusal to drink encouraged questions about their masculinity. Nowadays, the pressure is felt equally by girls. And since alcohol reduces sexual inhibitions, many unwanted pregnancies occur as a result of teen-agers having casual sex while high on liquor.

The adolescent and teen-age years are supposed to be a time of carefree fun. In our youth-oriented society, one's twenty-first birthday is no longer seen as the threshold of freedom; rather, it is more often seen as a sentence to the prison of adulthood—and to aging. Young people feel pressured to party, to enjoy the pleasures of adulthood without the responsibilities, to live now! More and more, the youthful peer group equates pleasure and fun with drinking, and an increasing number of young people, frightened of being outsiders, are falling into line.

SERIOUS EMOTIONAL PROBLEMS

An adolescent or teen-ager can have parents who drink, can have at least tasted liquor at an early age, and not become a problem drinker. An adolescent or teen-ager can drink with his or her parents' permission and not become a problem drinker. He or she can drink to overcome feelings of social inadequacy or because of a pessimistic attitude about the future and not become an alcoholic. He or she can also drink because friends drink and not become a problem drinker. But the more these influences combine, the more likely it is that the young person will become an alcoholic.

The most dangerous combinations are drinking to overcome feelings of inadequacy and to cope with pessimism about the future. Often, the adolescent or teen-ager who drinks for these combined reasons has serious emotional disturbances. Or, one reason alone may be so deep and intense that no other reasons are necessary. There are many sources for the serious emotional problems of young people. Perhaps their parents reject them for not fulfilling their expectations or the children reject their parents because they seem overprotective or unloving. Perhaps, if they are males, they feel a deep sexual inadequacy. Perhaps, if they are females, they are too afraid to assert themselves, are too passive. The point is, in the cases of such people, that drinking is not the basic problem. They would be emotionally disturbed anyway; alcohol just aggravates a situation that is already present. The trouble is that alcohol abuse can turn a minor emotional disturbance into a severe emotional problem, and this is much more true of young people than of adults. As mentioned earlier, adults have had the opportunity to develop many more coping mechanisms. Drinking may be only one of them. Since young people haven't had the same life experience, drinking may be one of the only coping mechanisms they have, and they rely heavily on it. According to one young person, whose comments echo those of many others:

> I had a hard time establishing my identity, you know, always felt inadequate. All the men around me—my Dad, my brothers—were so tough. I tried to be tough, too. I would only watch Westerns on TV. The men in those movies drank whiskey. I started to drink whiskey to be tough like them.

Some who have studied teen-agers and adolescents claim to have isolated the characteristics that foretell an eventual drinking problem. Certainly, if true, these findings are valuable. But they would have been much more valuable if they had been available ten years ago. With young people drinking at an increasingly younger age, it is becoming harder to distinguish problem drinking as the effect, as opposed to the cause, of their emotional disturbances. Only one thing is certain: The young person who becomes an alcoholic suffers from a much more severe emotional disturbance than does the adult alcoholic.

5

ALCOHOL AND THE BODY

Wine is at the head of all medicines;
where wine is lacking, drugs are necessary.—Babylonian Talmud, c. 450

A hot drink is as good as an overcoat.—
Petronius, c. A.D. 60

EARLY BELIEFS

When Arnaud de Villeneuve discovered the process of distillation in the 1300s, he was looking for a cure for every type of
sickness. When he produced alcohol he thought he had found
that cure, which is why he called it "the water of life." He
claimed it would make one live longer and that it was good for
the heart and all physical ailments. Word quickly spread to
other parts of Europe, and before long Europeans were drinking distilled alcohol in large amounts. Many believed that the
more they drank the healthier they would be.

The idea that alcohol was good for ailments and for the
health generally was not new. Fermented alcoholic beverages
had been used for medicinal purposes for centuries. The ancient Egyptians had some 100 medicines that included beer.

Ancient Greek and Roman doctors prescribed wine for many of their patients' ailments. Wine was an especially popular remedy for colds. It was believed that liquids first went into the lungs to moisten them and then passed on into the stomach. Wine, it was thought, relieved congestion in the lungs. The early Hebrews used alcohol as medicine and so did the early Christians. St. Paul gave this advice in one of his letters to St. Timothy: "Use a little wine for thy stomach's sake and thine other infirmities." Early European peoples used beer for coughs, hiccups, and breathing problems.

By the 1600s people realized that alcohol was not a cure for all diseases, but they still believed it was good for many ailments. The Europeans who settled in North America brought these ideas over with them, of course. Elderly people were given beer to help their arthritis. Children with stomachaches were dosed with blackberry brandy. Babies who cried too much were given rum mixed with water to make them drowsy. Anyone, no matter what age, who had a cold drank hot toddies, mixtures of rum or whiskey with honey or lemon juice and spices.

It was also believed that alcohol could help prevent disease. A healthy dose of liquor was given to anyone who had been out in the cold, or out in the sun, too long. Typhoid fever and malaria were common, and it was thought alcohol would prevent them. Both men and women started the day with a drink of wine or brandy, believing it would help their blood circulate better, clear their heads of drowsiness, and act to ward off disease.

The belief that alcohol was good for the health gave rise to one of the most common toasts. The phrase "to your health" clearly comes from the times when people believed the liquid they were about to drink was good for them.

In the 1800s alcohol was thought to be good for snakebites. And until ether was invented in the 1840s, alcohol was frequently used to dull pain during medical or dental operations. We all have seen Western movies in which a man takes a healthy swig of whiskey before a bullet is removed.

Considering that alcohol never did cure hiccups or remedy colds, improve the circulation or prevent malaria, it is amazing how long belief in its medicinal effectiveness persisted. It is almost as difficult to understand why so few people publicly suggested that alcohol might be harmful until the 1700s, and why so few people listened to those who did. Medicine *was* very primitive for centuries, and medical knowledge limited. Not until the late 1700s did belief become widespread that alcohol was harmful to the body. Dr. Benjamin Rush, a prominent physician and a signer of the Declaration of Independence, was convinced that hard liquor caused ailments of the liver and the throat, diabetes, and a number of other diseases, including madness, and in the 1780s he published a paper stating his theories. Today we know a great deal more about the effects of alcohol on the body, and though some of Dr. Rush's theories have been proved wrong (he thought alcohol ruined the texture of the hair), some have also been proved right (alcohol abuse does indeed cause liver disease). He pioneered the study of alcohol's effects on the body.

PRESENT KNOWLEDGE

> Wine is a poison which bores through the bowels.—William Scarborough, 1875

> It's all right to drink like a fish—if you drink what a fish drinks.—Mary P. Poole, 1938

As mentioned earlier, when alcohol is taken into the body it goes directly to the stomach, where it is absorbed into the stomach and small intestine and carried by the blood to the liver. The liver accepts the amount it is able to handle in the process of oxidation and· sends the rest back into the blood, which takes it to the heart, which pumps it back into the circulatory system, which carries it to all parts of the body. The percentage of alcohol in the blood depends on several things: the alcoholic content, or "proof" of the liquor, the amount of liquor consumed, the amount of time during which the liquor is consumed, whether or not there is food in the stomach, and the physical size of the drinker.

Many people feel that if they drink only beer or wine, they will not consume as much actual alcohol as they would if they drank whiskey. As a matter of fact, a can of beer, a glass of wine, and a shot of whiskey all contain about the same amount of alcohol, even though they differ greatly in volume.

Everybody knows that the more they drink the greater the percentage of alcohol there is in the blood. But there are differences among drinks that affect the rate at which the alcohol passes from the stomach and small intestine into the bloodstream. Water dilutes alcohol and slows the process of absorption. Beer contains a lot of water. Absorption is also slowed when whiskey is mixed with water but not when it is mixed with ginger ale or soda. Rather than slowing the process of absorption, carbonated liquids hasten it, for they contain carbon dioxide. Champagne contains carbon dioxide, which is the reason why it causes a "high" more quickly than regular wine. The fruit wines also contain carbon dioxide, which is why they are more intoxicating than beer.

It is common knowledge that people are less affected by liquor if they drink slowly than if they gulp drinks. This is because the liver has a set rate at which it can oxidize alcohol and a set amount that it can work on at one time. If a beer is sipped, the alcohol reaches the liver in manageable amounts, which are oxidized quickly. Relatively little is sent out into the bloodstream. If the same amount of beer is gulped down all at once, the liver cannot handle it, and a considerable amount goes into the bloodstream. It takes about two hours for the body to oxidize or otherwise eliminate the alcohol from one drink. Five drinks will take ten hours to oxidize completely. There is no way for the average person to speed up the process. Experiments with fructose, a sugar found in fruits and honey, show that injections of the substance into the veins can speed oxidation of alcohol, but the average drinker can hardly take advantage of the remedy. Common attempts to sober up, such as drinking black coffee, taking cold showers, or taking deep breaths of fresh air do absolutely nothing to speed the oxidation process.

"Never drink on an empty stomach" is an old and wise maxim. Food in the stomach, even if it is only milk, acts to dilute the alcohol, so that it is absorbed at a slower rate. Also, when there is food in the stomach, the liver is working to oxidize it, and the alcohol is taken into the liver along with the food rather than bursting in on it suddenly, as happens when there is no food in the stomach.

The size of one's body does indeed affect the amount of liquor one can hold. The larger (not fatter) the person, the more water his or her body contains. This body water acts to dilute alcohol. The reason why very fat people are an exception is that their extra weight is not water but fatty tissue, which doesn't do a thing to dilute alcohol. A small person cannot manage as much alcohol as can a large person. In fact, adults who encourage small children to drink because they think it is cute are endangering those children's lives. There have been cases in which youngsters have *died* after drinking a single glass of wine.

Liquor reaches and affects every part of the body. Too much liquor, taken over a period of time, can seriously impair the functioning of the bodily organs and can cause a variety of ailments and diseases.

The first area of the body liquor reaches is the digestive system. Heavy and sometimes even moderate use of alcohol can damage the lining of the stomach and small intestine, causing inflammation and quite frequently ulcers. Nausea and vomiting after too much drinking are usually the result of this inflammation, although nausea and vomiting can also result from the mixing of drinks. It is a popular belief that mixing drinks can increase the effects of alcohol. This is not so. All it does is make the drinker sicker, because the various chemicals in the drinks react upon each other *and* upon the stomach.

With increasingly heavy use of alcohol there may be damage to the nerve cells in the stomach and, as mentioned in chapter 1, to the stomach muscles. They lose tone, the rate of digestion is slowed, and food breakdown is hampered. Heavy use of alcohol can also damage the blood vessels in the tongue and cause it to become permanently swollen.

Diarrhea often results from excessive drinking, and it is thought that the various oils present in most alcoholic beverages provoke the condition. Chronic use of large quantities of alcohol can also cause disease of the pancreas.

The liver is the part of the digestive system that is most seriously affected by alcohol abuse. Cirrhosis of the liver is among the top ten causes of death in the United States. Cirrhosis is a condition of cell destruction, caused both directly and indirectly by intake of too much alcohol. While it is not clearly understood how, excessive amounts of alcohol cause the build-up of fat in the liver and destroy its cells, which are replaced by scar tissue. It becomes swollen in some parts and shrunken in others. The more fat and scar tissue present, the less the liver can function. Weakness, loss of appetite, weight loss, chronic indigestion, and constipation result, as well as hepatitis.

Cirrhosis of the liver is believed to result in part from malnutrition, which is why alcohol also causes the disease indirectly by deranging the appetite mechanisms, destroying the appetite for food. Alcohol calories provide energy, but they cannot be stored for future use, nor can they be used to build up body tissues. All they do is cause fat. Heavy drinkers can thus be overweight but malnourished in proteins, carbohydrates, vitamins, and the other essential substances that foods provide.

Alcohol intake also affects the circulatory system. One of the first effects a drinker notices is a warm, flushed feeling. This is because the blood vessels in the skin enlarge. Small doses of alcohol cause an increase in blood pressure and an increased heart rate. But this condition does not last long. Alcohol actually slows down the heart rate, causing less blood to be pumped throughout the system. Thus, alcohol is not beneficial to a person who is very cold. In fact, it is bad for the person because it slows the circulation rather than increases it and lowers the body temperature. In extreme cases, the cardiac nerves are paralyzed, causing instant death. Alcohol abuse contributes to a variety of heart diseases, the primary cause of death nationally.

Chronic heavy drinking causes the walls of the blood vessels to thicken, which accounts for the swollen, red appearance of the noses and faces of many alcoholics. This slows down the passage of blood through the vessels and thus hinders the carrying of nutritional materials to the body cells. Eventually, these cells deteriorate.

Alcohol reaches the brain and spinal cord through the blood. First it is carried to such higher brain centers as those that control speech, memory, and reasoning. It causes a decrease in the number and speed of the impulses transmitted back and forth from the body and brain, which is the reason inhibitions are reduced and, after too much drinking, a person may exhibit behavior totally unlike that of his or her sober condition, and have no memory of that behavior.

Next, alcohol reaches the brain's motor centers, which control speech muscles, movements, reflexes, etc. After too much alcohol, the impulses from the motor centers are reduced and slowed. Speech becomes slurred, the person staggers, vision becomes blurred, hands become shaky.

Then the alcohol hits the lower brain, affecting the breathing and the circulation. As mentioned earlier, excessive amounts of alcohol can cause heart failure by paralyzing the cardiac nerves. It can also paralyze the respiratory center of the brain, causing breathing to become slow and deep and possibly to cease altogether.

Prolonged, heavy drinking *destroys* brain cells, and the body cannot produce new cells in the brain. The optic nerve may be impaired, causing a loss of vision for both near and far objects. Cells of the motor system are damaged, affecting the reflexes and the movements of the voluntary muscles. Cells of the higher brain centers are killed, resulting in the inability to learn or to remember. Autopsies of chronic alcoholics have revealed massive destruction of brain cells. About 20,000 cells die in the brain with each bout of excessive drinking.

Young people tend to think of themselves as immortal. Age thirty seems light years away, and they cannot even imagine themselves as old. Since the diseases that have been described here generally occur over a long period of time—cirrhosis of the liver, for example, usually takes fifteen to twenty years to develop in adults—the young person with a drinking problem is not alarmed by the possible effects on his or her body. How can he or she relate to something twenty years off?

Unfortunately, alcohol does not take as long to damage young bodies as it does to affect adult bodies. Cirrhosis of the liver may take fifteen to twenty years to develop in an adult, but in a young person of fourteen it can occur in fifteen to twenty months! The bodily organs of adolescents and teen-agers are often not completely mature. Often they cannot handle the abusive effects of a large amount of alcohol as well as adult bodily organs. It was noted earlier that very small children have died after a single glass of wine or hard liquor. Their systems simply could not handle the liquor. This could not happen, say, to a twenty-five-year-old. Place adolescents and teen-agers on a continuum according to age between a child of five and a person of forty, in whom it has taken fifteen years for cirrhosis of the liver to develop, and figure the ability of the body of, say, a fifteen-year-old to handle liquor.

Being younger than adults, adolescents and teen-agers are also generally smaller. It has already been noted that larger people can hold their liquor better because they have more body water, and thus adults as a general rule can handle alcohol better than young people for this reason. Also, adult drinkers have had more experience with liquor than youthful drinkers. They have learned how to compensate for the slower reflexes, the difficulty in concentrating, and so forth, which accompany even moderate drinking. This is not true of young drinkers, which is an important aspect to consider, especially when it comes to drinking and driving. Studies have shown that even low concentrations of alcohol in the blood are a factor in teen-age driving accidents; among adults aged twenty-five to sixty-nine, the same low concentrations of alcohol are not a factor in auto crashes. Despite the insistence of some youthful drivers that their reflexes are quicker than those of adults, even when they have had a drink or two, that simply is not true.

A discussion about the effects of alcohol on the body cannot be ended without mention of the hangover. This common and highly unpleasant aftermath of drinking too much involves headaches, nausea, extreme thirst, sensitivity to bright lights and loud noises, and exhaustion. These symptoms are the result of poisoning by the drug alcohol. Headaches are caused by the substances in alcohol that have not been completely oxidized. The causes of nausea have already been discussed—it is generally the result of alcohol irritation to the stomach lining. Insatiable thirst occurs because alcohol causes some of the water in the body's cells to move out and into the spaces between the cells. Overreaction to lights and noises is a result of the sensitivity of the nerve cells in the brain. Exhaustion results from overactivity while under the influence of the energy-producing calories in alcohol.

Very little can be done to ease a hangover. It is a myth that a "hair of the dog," or more alcohol, will help. All it does is to act as an anesthetic by paralyzing the body's organs and masking the effects of the hangover for awhile. Some people drink hot beef bouillon, and there is evidence that the salt in the liquid does help a little, for the body produces a type of salt in its oxidation of alcohol. The best way to get over a hangover, unfortunately, is to wait it out. Aspirin, solid food, and bed rest in a quiet place are recommended. People suffering from hangovers are usually pretty quiet anyway, for not only are they feeling bad physically, they also are not feeling very good mentally.

6

ALCOHOL AND THE MIND

> Wine is first controlled by the character of the drinker, but gradually, as it warms the whole body and becomes mingled therewith, itself forms the drinkers character and changes him.—Plutarch, A.D. 97

> They who drink beer will think beer.—Washington Irving, 1818

Alcohol is a consciousness-changing drug. People use it to achieve different states of feeling or awareness, and it has been used for these purposes since ancient times and throughout most of the world. About 675 B.C. someone, probably Stasinus of Cyprus, wrote: "The gods made wine the best thing for mortal man to scatter cares." About 350 B.C. the following advice was given in the Old Testament: "Give . . . wine unto those that be of heavy hearts. Let him drink and forget his poverty, and remember his misery no more."

Today, people are still drinking for those very same reasons. There is a great deal of alcohol abuse among poor people. The effects of poverty can be so overwhelming that people lose all hope, and the only thing they can look forward to is a brief period of escape from their misery every now and then. In addition, there is evidence that prolonged chronic drinking makes people unable to try to improve their circumstances.

On the other hand, within the past few decades alcohol abuse has increased substantially among the higher economic classes; obviously poverty is not the only cause of depression and hopelessness.

Let us take a look at how the human consciousness is changed as a result of alcohol intake. First of all, it must be pointed out that consciousness is directly controlled by the brain; therefore the changes caused by alcohol are really physiological changes and ideally belong in the previous section about alcohol and the body. However, as many of the ways alcohol acts on the brain are unknown, it is easier to discuss the resulting changes separately.

When drinking begins, and alcohol starts to take effect in small amounts, feelings of happiness and general well-being usually occur. These feelings are due in part to the actual, physical effects of alcohol, but they can also be due to the expectations of the user. Studies have shown that if one group is given mixed drinks and another group is told it is being given alcohol but really drinks a beverage that contains no alcohol, some in the group that actually drank alcohol will show no effects at all, while some in the group that drank no alcohol will begin to act high. In actual social stituations, people who do act high earlier than the rest put pressure on those around them to drink more and faster so they can get high, too.

Those who get high suddenly have a great deal of energy, which accounts in part for using the word *high* to describe the feeling. They want to dance, or they become more talkative, or they laugh a lot. As mentioned in the previous chapter, this is partly a physiological reaction. Alcohol contains calories, which provide energy. Also certain of the brain's mechanisms are inhibited, resulting in the suppression of unpleasant feelings or anxieties, and hyperactivity of other portions of the brain. But partly, again, it is also psychological. Drinkers deceive themselves that they are happy and free from care.

Just as adolescents and teen-agers are affected more quickly by alcohol than adults because of their smaller size and greater inexperience with alcohol, so, too, they are more susceptible to psychological intoxication. But whether one is a teen-ager who has had two drinks or an adult who has had four, one is practicing self-deception under the influence of that amount of alcohol. When even slightly intoxicated, people tend to feel superior and not capable of wrongdoing or, especially, wrongthinking.

But if people who feel socially inadequate, particularly shy or painfully self-conscious persons, think alcohol will make them as energetic or as talkative or as funny as their normally more extroverted friends under the influence of alcohol, they will be disappointed. Studies have shown that alcohol affects outgoing people more than quiet people. Both can have the same blood alcohol level and still act very differently. Most of us probably know a normally outgoing person who becomes really obnoxious after a few drinks. The person who is normally quiet and introverted will be more relaxed and perhaps more talkative, but not as conspicuously high.

With a few drinks in them, people begin to have fantasies in which they are incredibly powerful. The plain-looking girl imagines herself being able to attract the handsomest and most popular boy. The boy who never seems to be able to say the right thing imagines putting down a more eloquent acquaintance with the perfect phrase. People under the influence of liquor often come up with what they believe are the most creative ideas—for a song, for an assigned paper, for an invention, even for starting a business.

They are encouraged to take chances. A youth under the influence of alcohol may take on larger and tougher opponents in a fight he would not seriously consider starting when sober. The same change has occurred in laboratory animals. Animals that will not go after food for fear of receiving an electric shock will overcome that fear under the influence of alcohol.

A girl who has had a few drinks may forget her fears of pregnancy or her usual ideas of morality, especially when her partner has acquired from alcohol the courage to be more insistent and has an inflated idea of his own sexual prowess. This is not true only of adolescents and teen-agers; it can be true of adults as well. It should be pointed out here that drinking may very well lower sexual inhibitions, but it does not improve sexual performance. In fact, it decreases it, since alcohol affects the central nervous system, causing nerve impulses to slow down. It also decreases muscle coordination. Both these factors are important in sexual activity. Alcohol may relax the will, but it also lessens the ability or, as Shakespeare said, "provokes the desire, but takes away the performance."

All these changes occur gradually from the beginning of drinking to the point when the "high" is highest. After that point is reached, drinkers begin to come down, to feel tired and sleepy. They get depressed and become more aware of their troubles; sometimes they even start to cry. This most often happens to people who were depressed to begin with and drank to overcome that state. Depressed people who drink to get out of depression may feel better briefly after drinking, but since they are likely to get even more depressed while still drunk, drinking can hardly be considered a good idea. A sizable number of suicides, or suicide attempts, can be directly linked to drinking. Accidents, too, are frequently linked with alcohol consumption.

One of the aftermaths of drinking is physical discomfort, such as extreme thirst, or a headache, or general bone-tiredness. At that point, being no longer in the euphoric high state, drinkers may believe they are sober, or nearly sober, once again, and feel able, for example, to drive home.

This is not true. While the level of alcohol in the blood may have begun to fall, it does so gradually, and it will be several more hours (the actual number depends on how many drinks have been downed) before it reaches the level of zero. Drinkers may be coming down psychologically, while being physically still quite drunk. They may have stopped laughing and talking and imagining themselves as powerful, sexy, artic-ulate, and so forth, but they still may have trouble walking without staggering or talking without slurring their words, and their reflexes and decision-making powers are far from nor-mal.

In most cases, drinkers fall asleep long before the blood alcohol level reaches zero and most of the effects of alcohol have worn off. Sleep, incidently, is something that drinkers' bodies almost force them to do. The familiar image of a drunk passing out while still drinking is an example of a bodily sur-vival mechanism. Sleep helps to prevent drinkers from literally drinking themselves to death, although there have been cases when comas and death have resulted from overdrinking—in adults as well as children.

The kind of sleep depends on the amount drunk earlier. A rousing drunk will, of course, result in a deep, "dead to the world" type of sleep. The average drunken experience will cause a restless and fitful night and feelings of tiredness and irritability the next morning.

Tiredness may be the least of the "morning after" discomforts. In fact, all of the physical effects of overdrinking that we generally think of when we think of a hangover may not be nearly as serious as the psychological hangover. The events of the previous night take on an entirely different aspect in the cold light of the following morning. The worries and fears, which alcohol masked for a few hours, return and are often accompanied by new ones. The nausea increases when the person remembers what he or she has said or done under the influence of alcohol. Worse still, the person may not be able to remember what happened at all! Such blackouts are familiar to people who habitually get drunk.

There is an interesting aspect to these blackouts. As the authors of an article entitled "Alcohol and Consciousness: Getting High, Coming Down" state:

> At a party late at night, you may tell a person about some terribly important matter that he or she will have forgotten by next morning. But the next time that person transcends into the alcohol state, he'll remember it perfectly. The same thing happens to certain chronic drinkers who forget where they hid their bottle until they're again as drunk as when they put it there in the first place.

This factor is one reason why alcohol is not considered a consciousness-changing drug.

For most people, it is very disquieting not to be able to remember their actions during the drunken state. They suspect their behavior to have been shameful or embarrassing, but unless they ask what happened, or someone reports it to them, they can only worry about it. One thing the drinker *can* often know exactly is just what great creative production occurred during the drinking experience. Frequently, drinkers will write down such ideas when they come to them. Students have been known to write entire papers while under the influence of alcohol, just as they have while high on marijuana or LSD. But the masterpiece of the night before generally seems pretty mundane the next morning. And if it is not mundane, then it is likely to be impossible to accomplish. The drinker who conceives a great idea for a business realizes when sober that he or she hasn't either the background or the experience or the money for something that seemed entirely possible the night before.

Many realize they were sexually indiscreet and are plagued with worry about the consequences. Or they may wake up in a jail cell or hospital, having been a perpetrator or a victim in an auto accident or in some other violent crime.

The foregoing description of what one who overdrinks experiences is somewhat familiar to everyone who has been drunk—even once. But there are major differences in the long-range results of occasional versus habitual intoxication. Chronic overdrinking leads to destruction of the brain cells, and studies have shown that severe alcoholics score very much the same on tests as people with brain damage do. This is especially true when in both cases the damage is to those areas of the brain that control judgment, learning from experience, ability to work toward a goal. In other words, some alcoholics no longer have the brain mechanisms to exercise good judgment, to learn from experience, and to be able to work toward the goal of kicking the alcoholism habit.

Alcoholics have been studied to see how damage to other parts of the brain affect their functioning. The common idea of a chronic drunk is that, among other things, he or she is no longer able to carry on an intelligent conversation. But studies have shown this is often not the case. The brain has two halves, or hemispheres. Among other things, the left hemisphere controls language. Among other things, the right hemisphere controls thought, the recognition of shapes, textures, space relationships between objects. According to the results of several studies, the left brain hemisphere seems to suffer less from years of heavy drinking than does the right hemisphere. So, an alcoholic may be able to speak very intelligently, but meanwhile his or her ability to think, to distinguish among objects by touch and sight, may be seriously impaired. Since these are unconscious mechanisms, an alcoholic may not realize that his or her ability to perceive is not what it once was.

The words *schizophrenic* and *psychotic* are frequently associated with the behavior resulting from the use of drugs such as LSD or speed, but less commonly used in connection with alcohol.

A lot of psychological jargon is thrown around so freely these days that many people use it without really knowing what it means. For example, someone can be very insecure without being paranoid. The following list is given to clarify terms as they are used here:

- A *psychosis* is a serious disorder of the mind.
- *Schizophrenia* is a term applied to forms of psychosis in which there is a separation of mental functions, often with the affected person assuming a second personality.
- *Delusions* are errors in judgment or perception, such as the idea that one has no stomach and thus refuses to take food.
- *Paranoia* is a form of fixed delusional insanity, usually of persecution.
- A *hallucination* is an error in perception affecting one of the sense organs, such as imagining seeing lights in pitch darkness or hearing one's name called when there is complete silence.

It is highly unlikely that the average adolescent or teen-ager or, for that matter, the average adult, has ever encountered many of the mental states defined above. But disorders called chronic psychoses can develop in people who consume even small amounts of alcohol, although it is likely that they were prone to serious emotional disturbances and behavior disorders to begin with. At any rate, in the state of intoxication, these people can experience confusion, disorientation, hallucinations, delusions, and very aggressive behavior for several hours.

A person can be a heavy user of alcohol over a long period without experiencing any serious mental disorders. Then, suddenly, a single episode of excessive drinking can bring on auditory hallucinations, delusions, marked fear or panic, and sometimes attempts at suicide. This state usually lasts between one and four weeks.

Then there are the psychological effects of withdrawal from the drug alcohol, when someone who is actually physically dependent on the drug is deprived of it. Daily usage of alcohol over many weeks or months in large and increasing doses causes the body to adapt to alcohol and actually to need it. Should alcohol suddenly become unavailable, or only available in smaller amounts, delirium tremens, commonly called DT's, occur.

DT's can also occur following a long course of drinking, which has ended in a bout; or the condition may be brought on by an injury or deep worries in a heavy drinker. First, there are tremors, or shakes, all over the body, especially in the hands and tongue. Then, there is no appetite, nausea sets in, the person is feverish and moves about at random. The hallucinations come. The person starts seeing things that are not there—spiders, flies, mice, rats coming out of the wall, or the floor. The terror of such an experience can lead to suicide or cause the person to withdraw into a state of permanent mental feebleness.

Paranoid psychoses can be speeded up by alcohol use. So can schizophrenia. Both disorders begin without the help of alcohol, but alcohol helps mask their symptoms and speed their progress. It is now believed that half of all first admissions and 40 percent of all admissions to state mental hospitals are alcohol related. Between 10 percent and 20 percent of the long-term patients in hospitals are there because of permanent psychoses from alcohol. This is 20 percent more than ten years ago.

Back in the 1780s Dr. Benjamin Rush decided that drinking caused madness. We now know that the roots of madness do not lie in alcoholism. But Dr. Rush was on the right track, for alcohol can cause both psychological and physiological loss of control over one's mind.

7

ALCOHOLISM

> First the man takes a drink, then the drink takes a drink, then the drink takes the man.—a Japanese proverb

> He had drunk his way down the ladder far more quickly than he had found his way up it.—P. C. Wren, 1941

TYPES OF ALCOHOLISM

Alcoholism is a progressive disease, although progression is not necessary. Simple social drinking may lead to one of the types of alcoholism; then again it may not. The same is true of the types of alcoholism. One may have alcoholism of the first kind without ever progressing to the second, but one may also advance gradually from the least serious to the most serious form. The study of alcoholism has resulted in a division of alcoholics into four basic categories.

The first type, called Alpha Alcoholism, is a purely psychological dependence on alcohol. The person depends on alcohol to relieve bodily or emotional pain. Drinking is excessive and usually occurs at times, in places, and with effects that break the rules of normal, social drinking. Even this stage is very serious in young people, since *any* alcoholic intake is excessive, abnormal, and dangerous for boys and girls who are still developing mentally and physically. Still, the person can go without alcohol if necessary, and can maintain a fairly normal life-style. There will be occasional absences from work or school, a tendency to tiredness and less productivity, and some of the nutritional deficiencies that result from the loss of appetite caused by overdrinking. There may be family problems due to the amount of money necessary to support the alcohol habit.

This type of alcoholism can develop into a more serious type. But it can also go on for forty years without progressing further. It is sometimes called "problem drinking," but when it is necessary to separate alcoholism into types, problem drinking is not a useful term, for it is also sometimes used to describe physical dependence on alcohol.

The second type is called Beta Alcoholism. It does not involve either psychological or physical dependence on alcohol, and yet it is more destructive to the body than the first type. It is in this type of alcoholism that cirrhosis of the liver, ulcers, and other ailments of the stomach, and damage to the nerves occur. The reasons for the kind of heavy drinking that leads to such physical damage, may be found in the customs of certain social groups, for example, a group in which men feel they must prove their masculinity by drinking to excess. The bodily damage usually occurs from a combination of the effects of alcohol and malnutrition, and the alcohol would not be as damaging if Beta alcoholics ate properly in the first place. Beta alcoholics have a shortened life expectancy, and tend to have poor family relations because of the financial and emotional demands of excessive drinking. Yet, if Beta alcoholics go on the wagon or are deprived of liquor, for some reason, they do not suffer from withdrawal symptoms, for they have not become physically dependent on alcohol.

In Gamma Alcoholism, the alcoholic becomes physically dependent on liquor. This means that the body's tissues, for which alcohol is normally an alien substance, become tolerant of alcohol and the processes that occur in the body's cells change to accommodate the constant presence of alcohol. In other words, certain biochemical changes take place in the cells, which make them *unable to function normally* unless alcohol is present. Gamma alcoholics can go without liquor for short periods, but soon their bodies begin to crave the needed alcohol. If still deprived, the body reacts violently. The alcoholic has *delirium tremens* and other withdrawal symptoms.

In Gamma Alcoholism a definite progression from psychological to physical dependence on liquor can be seen. Once the drinker has reached a state of physical dependence on alcohol, he or she must fight to control the need to drink. The need for a drink occurs at times and in places where drinking is not socially acceptable, or acceptable only in moderation. The alcoholic knows that school, job, or family relationship is at stake and yet cannot control the problem. Although it is not certain, Gamma Alcoholism is likely to be the most frequent type of alcoholism in the Anglo-Saxon countries, including the United States. It is the only type of alcoholism recognized by Alcoholics Anonymous.

Finally, there is Delta Alcoholism. In Delta Alcoholism the drinker cannot stay away from liquor for even a day or two without suffering withdrawal symptoms, although he or she can still control the amount drunk on any given occasion. It is the type of alcoholism found most often in France and some other countries where large amounts of wine are consumed. Interestingly, psychological dependence on alcohol is relatively low in these countries. This is because alcohol—wine, for example—is customarily drunk casually and with great frequency. People do not drink to relax, or get high, or escape from worry so much as they drink because it is the custom to do so and society accepts high alcoholic intake.

BEHAVIOR OF THE DRINKER PROGRESSING TO ALCOHOLISM

> "It wasn't the wine," murmured Mr. Snodgrass, in a broken voice. "It was the salmon." (Somehow or other, it never *is* the wine, in these cases.)—Charles Dickens, 1836

> You have a very special feeling about the value of liquor. Even the dregs left in other people's glasses must never be thrown down the drain.—Reformed Alcoholic, 1968

As Gamma Alcoholism is thought to be the most frequent type of alcoholism in the United States today, it is the type we will concentrate on in outlining the progression from moderate drinking to alcoholism, although some of the kinds of behavior described below are also common in the progression to other types of alcoholism. One thing fairly common to alcoholics is how they got there and what they go through once they are there, which is why Alcoholics Anonymous works for many people. Those in the program realize they are not alone, that others are suffering or have suffered just as they did.

The first signs of a drinking problem are when people begin to drink more than their friends on any given occasion and begin also to drink more often than those around them. Naturally, this leads to the next step: They get drunk more often, and thus they are more often noisy or aggressive or careless.

Their friends begin to talk among themselves and sometimes directly to the person about his or her drinking.

They begin to experience blackouts during drinking episodes. The next morning they cannot remember what they did or said, but are afraid to ask anyone who was with them because they will give themselves away. Afer awhile, they really don't want to know what they did or said the night before.

They begin to make excuses for their drinking to friends, and when the excuses don't work they become angry and defensive. They refuse to talk about their drinking, or even about drinking in general. They become very adept at finding the one subject another person does not want to talk about and bringing *it* up when the other person mentions drinking.

Meanwhile, they are also beginning to make excuses about problem drinking to themselves. They compare themselves to all their misconceived notions of who problem drinkers are and how they behave, and decide they can't possibly have a drinking problem. They point out to themselves that the alcoholic enjoys getting drunk; since they don't, it follows that they are not alcoholic. In reality, one of the signs of a true problem drinker is his or her extreme fear of getting drunk.

They tell themselves that they do not really need liquor and try to prove it by staying away from alcohol for a specified period—one week, two weeks. But long before the period is up they find themselves planning where and with whom they will have that first drink and what it will be. All they have shown is that they can keep from actually drinking for the specified period, not that they can control the desire for alcohol. The control becomes progressively weaker. They intend to have one drink and end up getting drunk.

They remind themselves that alcoholics are bums. *They* get good marks at school or hold down a good job; thus, they can't be alcoholics. This is another misconception. Plenty of alcoholics manage, barely, to function effectively.

They look at themselves in the mirror—no red, bulbous nose, no red veins showing beneath the skin. Speech and muscle coordination are fine, and they are reassured, believing that alcoholics have a certain look about them. But they do not necessarily. Alcoholics are not easy to spot.

They rationalize away their drinking behavior. Yet at the same time they act in ways they know are not normal. As much as possible, they begin to take their habit "underground." They sneak drinks, mask their alcohol with some other liquid, so those around them will not know they are drinking.

They have fights with their families, quarrels with their friends. They begin to be devious at school or on the job. They may even get into trouble with the law. They have accidents, are much more prone to colds, pneumonia, and a variety of other ailments and diseases.

They become withdrawn, loners. People around are perfectly willing to leave them alone because they seem very edgy and moody. They are indeed moody. Their emotions change suddenly, from ecstatically happy to deeply depressed. They either work like dynamos or don't do anything at all, and they do nothing at all with greater frequency. The less they do, the more they dream, and the dreams become increasingly ambitious. As one reformed alcoholic put it, "You can never quite take care of today. But you have great plans for tomorrow."

Finally, they enter the extreme state of alcoholism in which they have hallucinations, nameless fears and hatreds, neuroses and phobias, a complete rejection of reality. They cannot function in the everyday world, cannot hold a job or maintain a personal relationship. Drunken binges are frequent, and they compulsively hide bottles, so there will always be a drink around to mask the effects of a hangover. They will die before their time.

It's all quite frightening—but obviously not enough to prevent people from becoming problem drinkers or alcoholics. It is sad to know that so many people are throwing away their lives, but it is tragic that a growing percentage of them are adolescents and teen-agers.

THE SCOPE OF TEEN-AGE ALCOHOLISM

> A national study has found that 28 percent of the nation's teen-agers are problem drinkers.—*New York Times*, 1975

> The younger the age at which youth starts to use alcohol, the greater the chances that he or she will develop into a chronic alcoholic.—Louise Bailey Burgess, 1973

Alcoholism occurs in approximately one out of every ten persons who use alcohol. This means that in the United States there are about 10 million alcoholics. Since the epidemic of adolescent and teen-age alcoholism has been only recently recognized, there are no definite statistics on how many of these 10 million people are adolescents or teen-agers. One thing is certain: alcoholism is on the increase. In 1970, there were only about 6 million alcoholics; by 1975 that number had increased by 4 million, and it is certain that the increase in youthful alcoholism has much to do with that huge jump. Almost every expert and analyst in the country agrees that preteen and teen-age problem drinkers or pronounced alcoholics probably account for more than *1.5 million* of the 10 million total.

Of this number, probably the majority are aged fifteen and over, but there is evidence that a growing percentage of youthful problem drinkers are younger than fifteen. In 1973, the

National Council on Alcoholism found that the youngest alcoholics coming to their attention dropped from age fourteen to twelve. A study by the council, released in 1975, found that one-fourth of the thirteen-year-olds surveyed could be classified as moderate drinkers—those who drink lightly once a week, or occasionally more heavily. It is now not uncommon to find severe alcohol problems in nine- , ten- , and twelve-year-olds!

This is serious, no matter how you look at it, and there are a number of ways to look at it. It's bad for our society economically, for it overburdens our hospitals, many of which are supported by public taxes. Alcoholics are accounting for an increasing percentage of admissions to mental hospitals; and consider the victims of automobile accidents. Also, the more people drink, the more accidents they are likely to have in the home; and the more people who drink, the more suicide attempts there are. It is bad for our society socially, because alcohol-related crimes like assault and murder are on the increase. It bodes ill for the future of our society, for what society can progress and prosper if its youth have no future? We need intelligent, energetic young people, not young people whose bodies and minds are destroyed. Alcohol addiction is bad for society, but it is disastrous for the individual. The average adult alcoholic can expect to live about twelve years less than the nonalcoholic or nondrinker. There are no comparable studies on the life expectancy of teen-age alcoholics, but it is likely that the younger the alcoholic the shorter his or her life span. Nor does the young alcoholic have the same opportunities and potential that nondrinking teen-agers have. Forget sports; excessive drinking impairs breathing and coordination, the ability to concentrate, and physical energy. Forget getting good marks; alcoholism brings with it the inability to concentrate on studying, and most of a drinker's concentration is on when and from where the next drink will come. Love? Only with another alcoholic. As a rule, a moderate drinker or nondrinker will not have anything to do even with a problem drinker, much less an alcoholic. And a relationship with another alcoholic will not last long, for alcoholism is more destructive of love than any other problem. If an alcoholic is female, the risk of unwanted pregnancy is high, and she is in the worst condition to bear a child. Studies of children born to alcoholic mothers show that alcohol can interfere with the baby's development and can cause defects of the joints and heart as well as premature and abnormally small births. Whether male or female, the alcoholic will make the worst possible parent, for he or she is likely to be a child abuser, or at best a child neglecter.

The three young people described on the following pages didn't consider these facts. For reasons not completely under their control they literally "drank themselves sick," and alcohol is a very lonely sickness.

The first time a young man, whom we'll call Kevin, tried liquor he got drunk. He was about five years old, and his parents let him join their New Year's Eve party. They thought it was cute to see him staggering around and laughing about nothing in particular. They were middle-class people with the normal hopes for their son. If anyone had tried to tell them they were starting Kevin on the road to alcoholism they would have scoffed at the idea. Yet, that is exactly what they were doing.

For the next four years or so Kevin drank intermittently. Alcohol made him feel less inadequate, he would realize years later, though at the time he could not put his feelings into words. It was easy to get liquor at home, because his parents kept it on hand. He would sneak some and drink it alone in his room. By the time he was nine he had become so dependent on alcohol that he took scotch mixed with milk to school in his thermos. He did not tell his friends about his drinking habit, for they seemed too "goody-goody." The nuns at the Catholic school he attended did not suspect a thing—how could a nine-year-old possibly have a drinking problem?

Kevin was an altar boy at his family's church, and he started stealing altar wine. Once, before a confirmation ceremony, he drank some of the wine and got sick. In fact, he threw up on the altar. He tried to clean it up, but everything smelled of wine and vomit. One of the priests became suspicious but did nothing.

By the time he was fourteen, Kevin was drinking gin, other hard liquors, wine—anything but beer, which made him sick. He was just entering high school, and he needed alcohol to get up, to go to sleep, and to stop the delirium tremens he now suffered from most mornings. He needed so much liquor by now that he could not take as much as he needed from his parents. So he worked out an agreement with his next door neighbor, a college student. The neighbor was on drugs and needed money; Kevin gave his allowance to the neighbor, who purchased alcohol for him.

Kevin was fifteen when he shut himself in his room with a supply of liquor and refused to leave. He did not go to school or even to the dinner table. The only time he would go out was at night, to get cigarettes or more liquor. It was such a monotonous existence that he thought he would go crazy. He would cry for no reason. He would get up in the morning and take a drink and be unable to hold it down. He couldn't eat. He wanted to die.

A girl we'll call Yvonne first tasted liquor when she was five. Once again, parents introduced that first drink—tequila.

It was at a party at her house. She got very drunk. Yvonne did not drink habitually until the age of twelve. At the time, she was already in high school. Blessed with a very high IQ, she had skipped two grades in elementary school and thus was two years younger than the other kids in the freshman class.

She felt different, as if she did not fit in with the others, who considered her something of an oddity. Her teachers, impressed with her intelligence and mindful of her young years, treated her specially, which did not help her image with her fellow students. She was shy, introverted, and very unhappy.

According to Yvonne, 100 percent of the kids in the high school were drinking. Fights broke out between students who were high. Many just lolled around in class and made no effort to do their school work. Yvonne didn't much like what she saw, but at the same time drinking seemed to be a way to become accepted. So, at the age of twelve, she, too, started to drink.

Soon she was getting drunk nearly every day. She had no problem getting liquor. At first, she got it from fellow students, but after awhile she ceased to drink with them. She had found a friend in alcohol and she preferred to drink alone. She knew the people who ran the neighborhood liquor store; they sold her liquor whenever she wanted it.

Incredibly, the school officials did nothing about her drinking or that of the other students. In fact, they refused to recognize that a problem existed. It was 1972–1973, and they were concerned only about drugs. Narcotics agents were familiar figures at the school. A student could be reeking of alcohol, but the agents didn't care.

Yvonne drank cheap wine. She developed a liver problem within a year and a half. The pain was worst in the morning, but it could cause her to double over at any time. Aware that it might have something to do with her drinking, she went to a doctor without telling her family. The doctor told her bluntly that if she continued to drink her liver would simply fail on her. But his warning did not stop her.

It was not until he was thirteen that a boy we will call Luis started to develop a serious drinking problem. When he was younger, he would ask for sips of his father's beer, which the older man would give him. He admired his father and wanted to be like him, which is natural for a young boy. But as the years passed, Luis showed an uncommon desire to be like and with older people. He did not like to be around kids his own age, and since the older kids considered him too young he became a loner.

He took more and more sips of his father's beer, and after awhile he developed a craving for it. Every day he would steal a can or two from the refrigerator. He figured his father had so much in there he would never miss a couple of cans. Luis forced his sister, two years younger than he, to drink it, too.

The summer before Luis entered seventh grade, when he was thirteen, a man in his twenties moved into the neighborhood, and before long the two were good friends. They drank cheap wine and beer, which the man provided.

Luis would not consider trying drugs. He feared dope, of overdosing and dying. Yet, by the time he entered seventh grade in the fall, he had a serious alcohol habit. He was not alone. Many seventh graders in the school drank, and the back row in most classrooms was their particular territory.

Alcohol made Luis too weak for sports and too tired to concentrate on his schoolwork. He got so he didn't care about school, and because he had no self-control he became a behavior problem. He was kicked out of junior high school.

Meanwhile, he was deteriorating physically. He got hungry sometimes, but food made him nauseous. In order to be able to eat, he had to skip a day of drinking. He suffered from frequent dizzy spells.

One night when he was drinking a wine concoction with some friends, Luis vomited blood and it scared him. But to leave or to go to a hospital would have been a sign of weakness. He kept on drinking the wine mixture in order to feel better. When Luis told his father about the blood, the older man offered to take him to a hospital. Luis did not want to go. They got into a terrible fight, and Luis threatened his sister with a knife.

Ten years ago—even five years ago—these young people would have been exceptions in the area of alcohol and youthful drinking. They are no longer exceptions.

8

WHAT TO DO
ABOUT ALCOHOLISM

> Thou shalt abstain, Renounce, refrain!
> —Goethe, 1806

> There is a crying for wine in the streets; all joy is darkened, the mirth of the land is gone.—Old Testament, c. 725 B.C.

PROHIBITING ALCOHOL

The United States government once outlawed alcohol, in the form of the Eighteenth Amendment to the Constitution. It seems hard to believe, in the 1970s, that Prohibition could ever have been possible. Yet, it was strongly supported by many Americans who constituted, if not a majority, a very powerful and very vocal minority. Prohibition, which began officially in January 1920, did not come about overnight; its roots extended back to the post-Revolutionary War period, when Dr. Benjamin Rush began to publish his theories about the unhealthy effects of alcohol.

Rush's campaign against alcohol led to the founding of the first temperance societies in the United States. Located in the eastern part of the country, these societies aimed to end drunkenness, not drinking. They argued for temperate, or moderate, drinking—for medicinal reasons or at public dinners—and were against hard liquor like rum, rather than against wine or beer. Their campaigns against hard liquor were quite mild. While there was an awareness across America that alcohol in excess was not good, there was no strong effort to change the nation's drinking habits.

The most active campaign against liquor was begun about 1810 by a Connecticut minister named Lyman Beecher. Beecher was the father of Harriet Beecher Stowe, who wrote *Uncle Tom's Cabin.* He felt that the country was in danger of being taken over by undesirables, and he blamed drinking and gambling. He traveled around preaching against drinking, and his sermons were printed and distributed widely. Within ten years, he had helped to bring about a definite change in many Americans' attitudes about liquor. Employers stopped giving liquor to their workers, and farm hands often were no longer allowed their daily drinking break.

Encouraged, Beecher formed a group, which later came to be called the American Temperance Union. It was against the drinking of hard liquor, but it did not see anything wrong with wine, beer, or cider. The Union grew quickly at first, and by 1835 had over 1 million members. But gradually a split occurred in its membership. Some of the members were against *all* alcoholic beverages, and they managed to change the Union's pledge to one that banned even wine, beer, and cider. Obviously, the nation was not ready for such a hard line. Membership in the American Temperance Union dropped off.

Other temperance societies formed and became powerful enough in some states to push through laws that limited the quantities in which liquor could be sold. In 1851, Maine passed a true prohibition law, which banned the sale or making of liquor in the state; and in following years twelve other states were to do the same.

During the Civil War, the prohibition forces eased up on their fight against liquor. Most were also against slavery, and they concentrated more on that cause. But with the end of the war, they turned back to the liquor issue. They had lost a lot of ground. In most states that had passed prohibition laws, the laws had been repealed. Maine, Kansas, and North Dakota still had their laws, but illegal taverns and liquor-sellers operated as if there were no laws at all. Clearly, new tactics were needed if prohibition was to become a reality.

The Anti-Saloon League was formed in Oberlin, Ohio, in 1893. Its purpose was to bring about prohibition on the local and state and eventually the national level through political action. Politics had been used before, but in the states where prohibition laws had been passed it had always been an issue between political parties. The Anti-Saloon League vowed to support any candidate who might be friendly to their cause, regardless of which political party he belonged to. In the following years, candidates supported by the League were elected to office, and prohibition laws began to be passed, first on local and then on state levels. By 1913, the League felt confident enough to mark its twentieth anniversary with the slogan, "A Saloonless Nation in 1920."

Four years later, in 1917, the Sixty-fifth Congress convened in Washington, D.C. Among the members were a sizable number of pro-Prohibitionists, called "drys." This was the Congress that voted to declare war on Germany, bringing the United States into World War I. After that vote, laws were needed to put the country on a wartime basis. The production and distribution of food had to be regulated and the drys put a clause in the bill that would ban the production or sale of alcohol during the war.

The Congressmen who were against Prohibition, the "wets," did not want this clause in the bill. Yet they realized there might be enough "drys" in Congress to push it through. So, the "wets" came up with an offer the "drys" could not refuse. They agreed to let the Senate introduce a prohibition amendment to the Constitution.

In order to become a Constitutional Amendment, a resolution must first be passed by both the Senate and the House of Representatives. Then it must be voted on by the legislature of every state, and two-thirds of those legislatures must pass, or ratify, it by a majority vote. The "wets" were certain the prohibition amendment would never make it. And, to be doubly sure, they managed to get the "drys" to agree that the amendment would have to be ratified within seven years. They did not think the Eighteenth Amendment would have a chance.

As it turned out, the seven-year limit was no safeguard at all. The Anti-Saloon League had done its job well. The Eighteenth Amendment was quickly passed by both houses of Congress, and it was ratified by the required thirty-six states in just a little over a year. On January 16, 1919, the people of the United States learned that as of one year later all making or selling of liquor would be banned. The Prohibition forces were joyous. The amendment was called "God's present" to the country, and it was predicted that a new nation would be born. They could not have been more wrong. James Oglethorpe had great hopes when the British Parliament banned rum and brandy in his new colony of Georgia in the 1730s, but the Prohibitionists in 1920 did not learn from his experience.

As soon as it was clear that Prohibition would become a reality, those drinkers who could afford it began to buy up as much liquor as possible, while it was still legal to do so. But most did not have the money, and shortly after Prohibition went into effect, there was a great demand for liquor. Drinkers did not care if liquor was illegal. They wanted it, and they were determined to get it.

Naturally, there were plenty of people around to supply the

demand for bootleg liquor. People made it in their bathtubs. Farmers operated stills, or alcohol-making setups, in the woods. People near the borders of Mexico and Canada bought liquor in these countries and smuggled it back. Those with boats rowed or motored or sailed out beyond the three-mile limit, which marked the end of United States territorial waters, and bought illegal liquor from larger boats anchored there. The area came to be called Rum Row. Their owners went to Europe, Cuba, and the West Indies, loaded up with as much hard liquor as the boats could hold, and then sailed back to just outside the three-mile United States boundary. From there they sold their liquor, making a handsome profit.

Drinkers were willing to pay prices that were double, triple, and more than the prices for which liquor had sold before Prohibition. Barely was the ink dry on the Eighteenth Amendment when illegal liquor became big business.

There is no doubt that Prohibition gave organized crime its big break. Before Prohibition, mobsters operated smuggling and dope and prostitution rings, but the money to be made in such activities was peanuts compared to the fortunes that could be reaped from the bootleg liquor industry. Soon, a highly organized underworld network crisscrossed the nation, including factories where illegal liquor was manufactured, delivery routes, and distribution points. A number of different gangs controlled specific areas in each city, and as long as they did not try to take over each other's territory they existed peacefully side-by-side. There was so much money to be made in the bootleg business that there was more than enough to go around.

The amount of alcohol Americans drank increased to a marked degree during Prohibition. Legal bars, which had closed when alcohol was outlawed, were replaced by double the number of illegal bars, called "speakeasies." During Prohibition, two segments of the population, which had not been particularly prone to drinking before, joined the ranks of America's drinkers. They were women and young people.

Alcohol, made illegal, became very attractive, and bootleg liquor was being consumed everywhere in increasing quantities. No party was complete without it. Wealthy and famous people rubbed elbows with gangsters, who had a very romantic image in the early days of Prohibition. The hint of danger they represented made drinking even more exciting. It became fashionable to thumb one's nose at the law. Women were just beginning to break away from the home, to get jobs, to demonstrate for the right to vote. Some saw drinking as a way to show their independence. And of course, many young people traditionally assert their independence by flouting the rules of adult society.

The law, meanwhile, was having great difficulty enforcing Prohibition. There were never enough federal agents to do the job, and local police departments and governments all too often were willing to look the other way in exchange for bribes. Very few speakeasies were unknown to the law. Many were such fly-by-night operations that by the time a raid against them was organized they had moved to other quarters. Some of the larger speakeasies had agreements with law enforcement agencies and were not bothered as long as they kept their operations peaceful.

Plenty of arrests were made, but more might have been made if the courts and jails had been able to handle them. No preparations had been made for the violators of the Prohibition law before it went into effect. As a result, within three years the population of the federal prisons had doubled and the courts were overrun with thousands of cases, which they did not have the time or the judges to handle.

Prohibition brought much violence to the United States. Unscrupulous or ignorant people tried to make whiskey out of methyl alcohol or wood alcohol, hair tonic or rubbing alcohol, even automobile antifreeze. As a result, thousands were poisoned and went blind or died. Thousands more were crippled because they drank a bootleg whiskey containing Jamaica ginger, a substance that caused paralysis of the legs and feet. This violence did not cause great concern, because it occurred here and there and was usually reported in the back pages of newspapers.

Of greater concern was the violence within the underworld over illegal liquor. Until the late 1920s, the bootlegging business was so good that there was plenty of territory and money for all the gangs. But as the years passed, some of the gangs grew hungry for an even bigger share of the territory and the profits. On February 14, 1929, on Chicago's North Side, five gangsters machine-gunned seven members of a rival gang in a struggle for control over bootlegging operations in the area. The St. Valentine's Day Massacre, as it came to be called, shocked the nation. People began seriously to question a law that caused such violence. The clamor for repeal grew louder when gang fighting increased and not just hoodlums but innocent bystanders were killed. In 1932, Prohibition repeal was an issue in the presidential election. In his campaign for reelection, Herbert Hoover pledged to try to make the Prohibition law, which he called a "noble experiment," a better one. His Democratic opponent, Franklin D. Roosevelt, promised that the law would be repealed. Roosevelt won the election in 1932, and it is safe to say that part of the reason was his stand on Prohibition.

Soon after Roosevelt was sworn into office, the Twenty-first Amendment to the Constitution, which called for repeal of the Eighteenth Amendment, was passed by both houses of Congress and sent to the states for ratification. A year later, the required number of states had done so and Prohibition was over, to the great relief of the majority of the nation.

Alcohol became less expensive when it was once again legal, and organized crime, after a period of conducting its old, minor rackets like prostitution and gambling, found a new gold mine in narcotics. Most of the former violence associated with liquor ended. But drinking continued at pretty much the same level as during Prohibition, which for the middle class, women, and young people, was at a higher level than before Prohibition.

Prohibition taught the United States an important lesson: The problem of alcohol abuse cannot be solved by outlawing alcohol. In fact, forcibly depriving a population of alcohol seems to encourage a larger percentage of that population to start drinking. Mark Twain was right when he wrote in 1889: "The thing that you can't get is the thing that you want, mainly."

THE ROLE OF PARENTS

> As each one wishes his children to be, so they are.—Terence, 160 B.C.

> I think parents should be very harsh about drinking. I wish they could have stopped me so I wouldn't have a drinking problem now.—Teen-age alcoholic, 1974

During the earlier discussion of why young people drink, it was pointed out that the most important reason was not for the effect, or because of peer group pressure, but because of parental influence. If parents are such a strong influence on the use of alcohol by young people, it follows that they can also be a strong influence on the nonuse or limited use of alcohol by young people, as statistics have indicated. If none of the parents in the United States drank, then neither would most of their children.

The problem, of course, is that a majority of parents in the United States do indeed drink, and they see nothing wrong with it. With respect to their children drinking, some of these parents are extreme in their attitudes and reactions. Some actively encourage their children, particularly their sons, to drink. They feel their children will be able to handle liquor if they practice a lot. Or, they feel their sons are showing early signs of manhood by wanting to drink at a young age; or their daughters will not be popular with their friends if they do not drink. Others actively discourage drinking by their children. Their attitude is the old "do as I say, not as I do" syndrome. Both groups are betraying their children, actually encouraging them to develop drinking problems. The first group openly invites the problems. The second group is so hypocritical about drinking that their children are likely to turn to alcohol out of spite.

In between these groups fall the vast majority of drinking parents. They do not feel there is anything wrong with their own drinking. They see no harm in letting their children taste their cocktails or the foam from their beers when their children are young. Once their children reach adolescence and early teen-age, they have a different reaction and frown on the same sampling of drinks that was cute a few years before. By the time their children are sixteen or seventeen, the parents' attitudes begin to change again. While they might not be too happy about their children drinking, they are relieved that the problem isn't more serious—after all, their sons and daughters could be on drugs. Also, they realize that in a year or two it will be legal for their teen-agers to drink and thus wonder how forceful they should be against drinking. When their children reach the age of eighteen, some parents celebrate the event by taking them out to a place where drinks are served. Some begin to ask their sons and daughters to join them in before-dinner cocktails or after-dinner brandies. Even those who let the event pass unheralded, know it is an important turning point. Usually, these parents feel rather relieved when their kids reach drinking age. They feel they are no longer charged with the responsibility of keeping them from becoming prob-lem drinkers. In reality, of course, their children may be on the road to alcoholism, or already alcoholics, by the time they reach eighteen.

Too often, drinking parents unwittingly encourage their children to drink by having such changeable attitudes about drinking. Kids need clear, firm rules and boundaries. If they don't have them, they feel insecure, and sometimes they turn to drinking because of this insecurity. Kids do not manage very well when they constantly receive conflicting signals.

If questioned about it, probably the majority of under-age drinkers would say they felt their parents should take a lenient attitude toward their drinking. But some would say they wished their parents were more strict about it, and probably a number of the majority secretly or subconsciously feel the same way.

The ideal drinking parent does not, first of all, abuse alco-hol him- or herself—does not get high or drunk, particularly in front of the children. The ideal drinking parent does not think it is fun to offer a very small person a taste of alcohol, or cute to see a child slightly high or drunk. The ideal drinking parent treats drinking like owning a car, marrying, or staying out until two o'clock in the morning. There are certain privi-leges that go with adulthood for a reason. Certainly, being twelve or fourteen years old doesn't automatically mean a person could not handle these privileges. But, as a general rule, he or she hasn't the experience, not to mention the physical, mental, or material capacities, necessary to deal with the responsibilities that accompany these privileges. Heaven knows, there are plenty of adults who can't deal with them!

In other words, "Yes, we drink, but we do not feel you should yet. Wait until you've had a little more time to come to know yourself, to find out who you are and how you feel about yourself, other people, material things. Sure, you can have a sip of our drinks, but you cannot have a drink of your own, and if we find out you have been drinking you will be disciplined. We realize your friends drink, but your friends are not you. *You* are *our* son/daughter. Use us as an excuse not to drink if you like—at first—but try to make it your own choice. If your friends are worth having, they will accept it."

The ideal drinking parent then trusts his or her children not to drink. If there is evidence that the children are indeed drinking, then whatever disciplinary action the parent has mentioned should be taken. If there is evidence that the youth has a serious drinking problem, the parent must take the hardest and most painful action of all—no action. Youthful alcoholics or problem drinkers are just like their adult counterparts—they are highly defensive. Punishment, nagging, even heart-to-heart talks simply don't work. The ideal parent first understands alcoholism and then understands that the only one who can help an alcoholic is the alcoholic.

UNDERSTANDING ALCOHOLISM AS A TREATABLE DISEASE

> A disease which neither needle nor medicine can reach.—Chinese proverb

> If we take habitual drunkards as a class, their heads and their hearts will bear advantageous comparison with those of any other class.—Abraham Lincoln, 1842

Though Dr. Benjamin Rush held some incorrect theories about the harmful effects of alcohol, it is interesting to note that he referred to excessive drinking of hard liquor as a "disease" and an "addiction." He was the first to estimate the rate of death by alcoholism in the United States as at least 4,000 per year in a population of less than 6 million. However, while his theories about what distilled alcohol did to the body and mind were accepted by some, his ideas that alcohol was a disease did not gain much attention. In general, until the nineteenth century, alcoholism was considered at worst a crime and at best a sin. People who became drunk were considered to be of low morality, and the common way to treat them was to put them in jail. As a general rule, this did not solve the problem. While some people were so embarrassed about waking up in a jail cell that they never got drunk again, most simply continued their excessive drinking and were in and out of jail for the rest of their lives.

Early in the 1800s, some medical men began to suspect that alcoholism might not be so much a moral lapse as an actual, treatable disease. Interestingly, those who held such theories were frequently doctors in mental institutions. Many of the patients in those institutions were there for alcohol-related reasons, and some doctors noticed there was a difference between these patients and the others. In 1828, Eli Todd, the head of the Hartford (Connecticut) Retreat for the Insane, even suggested that a separate hospital should be set up for the treatment of drunkards. However, understanding of alcoholism had not progressed sufficiently for Todd's suggestion to be taken very seriously. Not until 1868 was such a hospital established, the Washingtonian Home for the Fallen in Boston. Clearly, by this time a more sympathetic attitude toward alcoholism had become more widespread. Had Todd been successful in setting up his hospital forty years earlier, it most likely would have included the word *drunkards* in its name. "The Fallen" was a softer term for people in a chronically drunken condition. The words *alcoholism* and *alcoholic* are not really euphemisms at all; in fact, they are more accurate than terms used earlier, for they refer to a disease, a condition of illness.

The development of psychiatry in the nineteenth century contributed greatly to the acceptance of alcoholism as a disease, and the theory that alcoholism is the result of emotional problems is still generally accepted. But recently the theory has been advanced that alcoholism, while perhaps the result of emotional and personality disorders in some cases, may also have a physical basis.

Each person is an individual biochemically. This means that people differ in terms of blood composition, enzyme levels, gland activity, response to chemicals, nutritional needs, etc. Some people have to go to the bathroom more often than others. Some people perspire a lot; some people do not. Some people are allergic to penicillin, or to pollen, or to milk, or to grass. Some people attract mosquitoes; others do not. One person can stumble into a patch of poison ivy and break out into a rash; another person can do the same thing and have no reaction whatsoever. These differences are due to biochemical individuality.

In recent years, it has occurred to some doctors and medical researchers that the fact of biochemical individuality should be taken into account when trying to find the reasons for alcoholism. When a chemical substance affects a person, it is because this chemical substance interacts with the substances and mechanisms of that person's body. If the same chemical has a different effect on two different people, it must be due to their biochemical differences. Research into this theory is still in progress, but at some point in the future scientists may be able to isolate particular bodily substances and mechanisms that contribute to alcoholism. They may find that alcoholism is a result of individual body chemistry, for some people at least.

Other researchers are studying nutrition, especially inherited bodily characteristics and their influence on nutrition, in an attempt to understand the reasons for alcoholism. Because of these characteristics, a person may have an abnormally high need for certain nutrients, such as vitamins, minerals, and amino acids—a need that is not satisfied by the average diet. When this person drinks a considerable amount of alcohol, he or she creates a nutritional deficiency. The body's cells do not get needed nutrients, and malnourished cells in the tissues of the hypothalamus can damage the normal hunger mechanisms. In other words, the hypothalamus, which regulates hunger for needed nutrients, can become confused and require alcohol instead. When this happens, the need to drink is beyond the control of the individual, who can want to stop drinking mentally, but whose body demands alcohol.

Experiments have been done in which several rats in a cage are given a standard diet plus alcohol. Sometimes one rat or two will develop a habit of drinking large quantities of alcohol. Researchers have been able to cause these rats not to crave alcohol by increasing the amounts of certain nutrients in their diets. Rats and humans may not react in identical ways, but some very favorable results have come out of the nutritional approach to alcoholism—keeping alcoholics on a good basic diet, with nutritional supplements.

These theories about the physiological bases of alcoholism do not rule out the possibility of psychological bases. In fact, most theorists believe alcoholism is the result of a combination of physiological and psychological factors.

There is still so much we do not know about what causes alcoholism. What we do know for certain is that it is a disease. Directly or indirectly it causes more deaths than cancer, and the toll it takes on human lives—the pain, bitterness, and frustration it creates—is immeasurable. Too many people still view alcoholism as a moral failure, which only makes the problem of alcoholism in our society worse.

ALCOHOLICS MUST HELP THEMSELVES

> Every man shall bear his own burden.
> —New Testament, A.D. 60

> Against Diseases here, the strongest Fence,
> Is the defensive Virtue. Abstinence.—
> Benjamin Franklin, 1742

An alcoholic or problem drinker cannot be helped unless he or she wants help. This is one of the most frustrating facts about alcoholism. Arguments, coercion, even love cannot force a problem drinker to seek treatment. The reasons alcoholics do seek help are as numerous as the problem drinkers themselves. Some have to vomit blood in order to become sufficiently frightened to seek help. Others must hurt someone they love severely before they recognize their problem. Still others have to experience the shame of passing out or making fools of themselves in a public place before they will admit to alcoholism. And some seek help only after they have directly or indirectly caused a death. There are some who can go through all these experiences and still continue to drink, but the majority of alcoholics are capable (if the necessary brain mechanisms are not affected) of the sort of mental "click!" that causes them to say, "This is it. I've got a serious problem. I need help."

To date, the most successful way to deal with alcoholism is for alcoholics to aid one another by forming self-help organizations. Of these organizations, the oldest and most effective is Alcoholics Anonymous. AA was formed in 1935 by two former alcoholics, an Ohio doctor and a New York stockbroker. They began to go around the country talking openly about their experiences with alcoholism and encouraging alcoholics to talk about their problems. They brought alcoholism "out of the closet," so to speak, and helped people to face the problem openly and honestly, which is the first step toward its solution.

Basically, Alcoholics Anonymous is a kind of group therapy. People share their experiences, learn that these are common to many alcoholics, and receive support from the only people who can truly understand what they are going through —other alcoholics. Today, the organization has about 500,000 members in local chapters across the country. In addition to groups of alcoholics, the AA also sponsors Alateen programs for the children of alcoholics and Al-Anon Family Groups for the families of alcoholics. With the rise of teen-age alcoholism, special AA chapters just for young alcoholics have been formed, and more are being established every day. Many of these chapters are formed in association with the youth services division of the local police department or with community health care services.

While the group approach to alcoholism is successful for many alcoholics, the problem is still an individual one. Alcoholics Anonymous operates on the theory that the only cure for alcoholism is total abstinence. It is an extremely hard decision not to take another drink and a very difficult task to stick to that decision. Many new members of AA do not see how they can possibly face a life without alcohol. How can they go to parties or restaurants, or even watch television or read magazines, without being constantly exposed to alcohol and reminded that they are oddities in a drinking society? It is an exhausting and trying process to go on the wagon for good and AA, recognizing this difficulty, stresses a one-day-at-a-time approach. Of course, there is always the danger of relapse, of a drinking binge—after which the person has to start all over again. Yet many do manage to kick their addiction to alcohol—and nothing takes more courage or more will power.

Recently the theory has been advanced that alcoholics may not have to abstain totally from alcohol for the rest of their lives. If experiments concerning alcohol and nutrition are successful, then a former alcoholic may be able to take a drink now and then, provided he or she maintains a good diet and keeps taking nutritional supplements. Experiments are also being made using a chemical approach to alcoholism. Drugs like lithium are prescribed for the depression that a person might otherwise try to relieve with alcohol. A former alcoholic may be able to drink moderately without fear of going on binges as long as he or she is on lithium. Naturally, there is a lot of hope among alcoholics that alcoholism can be "cured" without total abstinence. It would be so much easier for alcoholics if they could overcome their penchant for alcohol abuse and join the ranks of the moderate social drinkers. Experiments in this area are still new and their success is open to challenge and criticism from many experts. For the time being, at least, the Alcoholics Anonymous approach is the most reliable and proven one. Yet there is some evidence that a less rigid approach may be possible.

The three teen-agers whose development of alcoholism was described in the previous chapter joined AA or similar programs. Kevin was lucky to have parents who cared enough about him to let him seek help on his own. They were very anxious about him, and their natural impulse was to force him to get help. But they were counseled not to make themselves an excuse for Kevin's drinking, and they heeded that advice. When he locked himself in his room with his liquor they did not try to make him come out. Instead, they began to leave slips of paper around, on which were telephone numbers where he could get help. After three months of constant drinking, mentally miserable and physically decimated, Kevin called one of the numbers. Immediately, someone came and picked him up and took him to a youthful alcoholism program. He was fifteen years old.

By contrast, Yvonne was forced into a program. She had become a behavior problem at school and became violent when she could not get a drink. Her parents and the school authorities cooperated in finding and taking her to a place where she could get help.

Fortunately, Yvonne came to agree that she needed to be in the program. Secretly, she was very frightened that she was going to die, for her liver gave her such pain. She received medical treatment for her liver and mental therapy in the form of group discussions with other teen-agers with drinking problems. Though still very shy, she began to discover that she was not so different and that the problems that made her seek escape in liquor were shared by many other teen-agers. Still, Yvonne's chances for success might have been better if she had made the initial move to enter the program herself.

The mental "click!" that caused Luis to join a teen-age alcoholism program occurred when, during the fight with his father about going to the hospital, he threatened his younger sister with a knife. He was disgusted with himself—his drinking had nearly made him injure his own sister! At the same time, he was terrified about what had happened to his body that was causing him to vomit blood. He consented to going to the hospital, and from there he went on to join a program recommended by the hospital.

Kicking the habit will not be easy for any of these teen-agers. In fact, it probably will be the hardest thing they will ever do in their lives. The first months were the hardest for them. They had to go to school, where everyone else was drinking and smoking pot. It was hard being the only nondrinkers in their crowd. It was almost unbearable to think about never drinking again. They were advised not to think about this to prevent its becoming an obsession. They found that the best way was to take one day at a time, and with each passing day they found it just a bit easier to deal with their problem.

Society could make things a lot easier for these kids and for adult alcoholics. There is still a stigma attached to alcoholism in our society. While we profess to have an enlightened view of alcoholism as a disease that can happen to anyone, many of us still regard alcoholics, even former alcoholics, as somehow weaker or less moral than nonalcoholics. Alcoholics are ridden with anxiety and shame. It is significant that the largest organization for alcoholics is called Alcoholics *Anonymous*. Solving the problem of alcoholism in the United States is not up to the alcoholics alone. The rest of society also has a responsibility to understand what alcoholism is all about.

Many readers may have evaluated correctly the statements made in chapter 1. But those who did are in the minority. A government survey has shown that 81 percent of the high school and 80 percent of the adult population of the United States believe that mixing drinks increases the effects of alcohol. Seventy-five percent of the young people and 65 percent of the adults surveyed were convinced that beer is less intoxicating than whiskey mixed with water.

The best way for both alcoholics and nonalcoholics to do something about this problem of alcoholism is to recognize and understand what the problem is. It is particularly important for young people to do so. Young people are the future, and if the epidemic of teen-age and adolescent alcoholism continues to increase, what kind of future can we look forward to? A nation of alcoholics, a nation that does not progress, a wasted future. True? Or false?

APPENDIXES

NATIONAL COUNCIL ON ALCOHOLISM, INC. DIRECTORIES

ALASKA

Anchorage — Anchorage Council on Alcoholism
P.O. Box 506
Anchorage, Alaska 99501
Tel: (907) 272-6211

ARIZONA

Phoenix — NCA-Greater Phoenix Area
Community Service Building
1515 East Osborn Road - Room No. 43
Phoenix, Arizona 85014
Tel: (602) 264-6214

CALIFORNIA

Carmel — Monterey Peninsula Council on Alcoholism
P.O. Box 1058
Carmel, California 93921
Tel: (408) 624-2256

Los Angeles — Alcoholism Council of Greater Los Angeles
2001 Beverly Boulevard
Los Angeles, California 90057
Tel: (213) 380-0332

Oakland — NCA-Alameda County
431 30th Street
Oakland, California 94609
Tel: (415) 834-5598

Pasadena — Pasadena Council on Alcoholism
201 North El Molino, Suite 107
Pasadena, California 91001
Tel: (213) 795-9127

San Diego — NCA-Greater San Diego Area
P.O. Box 20852
San Diego, California 92190
Tel: (714) 234-7381

San Francisco — NCA-San Francisco Area
2340 Clay Street - Suite 407
San Francisco, California 94115
Tel: (415) 346-1480

Santa Barbara — NCA-Santa Barbara Area, Inc.
804 Santa Barbara Street
P.O. Box 28
Santa Barbara, California 93102
Tel: (805) 966-6474

COLORADO

Colorado Springs — NCA-Pikes Peak Region, Inc.
P.O. Box 395
Colorado Springs, Colorado 80909
Tel: (303) 634-3487

Denver — NCA-Mile High Area
United Way Service Center - Room 506
1375 Delaware Street
Denver, Colorado 80204
Tel: (303) 623-6146

Grand Junction — NCA-Mesa County, Inc.
610 Rood
Grand Junction, Colorado 81501
Tel: (303) 243-3140

CONNECTICUT
   Cos Cob — Alcoholism Council of
      Southern Connecticut, Inc.
   521 Post Road
   Cos Cob, Connecticut 06807
   Tel: (203) 661-9011

DISTRICT OF COLUMBIA
   Washinton, D.C. — Washington Area
      Council on Alcoholism and Drug
      Abuse
   1330 New Hampshire Avenue, N.W.
   Washington, D.C. 20036
   Tel: (202) 466-2323

ILLINOIS
   Chicago — Chicago Council on
      Alcoholism
   6 North Michigan Avenue   Suite 1422
   Chicago, Illinois 60602
   Tel: (312) 726-1368

IOWA
   Des Moines — NCA-Des Moines Area, Inc.
   1223 Bankers Trust Building
   Des Moines, Iowa 50309
   Tel: (515) 244-2297

KANSAS
   Topeka — NCA-Kansas Division, Inc.
   2044 Fillmore
   Topeka, Kansas 66604
   Tel: (913) 235-2339

LOUISIANA
   Shreveport — Caddo-Bossier Council
      on Alcoholism and Drug Abuse
   Commercial Building - Room 9
   509 Market Street
   Shreveport, Louisiana 71101
   Tel: (318) 425-1403

MARYLAND
   Baltimore — Baltimore Area Council on
      Alcoholism
   22 East 25th Street
   Baltimore, Maryland 21218
   Tel: (301) 366-5555

MICHIGAN
   Detroit — Greater Detroit Council on
      Alcoholism
   6131 West Outer Drive
   Detroit, Michigan 48235
   Tel: (313) 864-4065

   Flint — NCA-Greater Flint Area, Inc.
   202 E. Boulevard Drive - Suite 300
   Flint, Michigan 48503
   Tel: (313) 235-0639

   Lansing — Tri-County Council on
      Alcoholism and Addictions
   300 No. Washington Avenue - Suite 304
   Lansing, Michigan 48914
   Tel: (517) 482-3392

   Muskegon — Muskegon County Council
      on Alcoholism
   308 Michigan Theatre Building
   Muskegon, Michigan 49440
   Tel: (616) 722-1931

MINNESOTA
   St. Paul — Family Service of St. Paul
   300 Wilder Building
   5th and Washington Street
   St. Paul, Minnesota 55106
   Tel: (612) 222-0311

MISSOURI
   Kansas City — NCA-Kansas City Area
   6155 Oak Street
   Kansas City, Missouri 64113
   Tel: (816) 361-5900

St. Louis – Greater St. Louis Council
on Alcoholism
1210 Locust Street - Room 101
St. Louis, Missouri 63103
Tel: (314) 231-9600

NEBRASKA

Lincoln – Lincoln Council on
Alcoholism
2ʟ7 Lincoln Center
215 South 15th Street
Lincoln, Nebraska 68508
Tel: (402) 475-2695

NEW JERSEY

Montclair – NCA-North Jersey Area,
Inc.
Council of Social Agencies Bldg.
Room 211
60 South Fullerton Avenue
Montclair, New Jersey 07042
Tel: (201) 783-9313

Red Bank – Alcoholism Council of
Monmouth County, New Jersey,
Inc.
54 Broad Street - Room 225
Red Bank, New Jersey 07701
Tel: (201) 741-5203

NEW MEXICO

Albuquerque – Albuquerque Area
Council on Alcoholism, Inc.
229-B Truman Street, N.E.
Albuquerque, New Mexico 87110
Tel: (505) 268-6216

NEW YORK

Buffalo – Buffalo Area Council on
Alcoholism
1 West Genesee Street
723 Genesee Building
Buffalo, New York 14202
Tel: (716) 853-0375

Corning – Corning Area Council on
Alcoholism, Inc.
Corning Hospital
176 Denison Parkway East
Corning, New York 14830
Tel: (607) 962-5051 (ext. 311)

Elmira – Chemung County Council on
Alcoholism
114 East Gray Street
240 Elmira Theater Building
Elmira, New York 14901
Tel: (607) 734-1567

Garden City – Long Island Council on
Alcoholism
350 Old Country Road
Garden City, Long Island, New York
11530
Tel: (516) PI7-2606

New York City – National Council on
Alcoholism - New York City
Affiliate
225 Park Avenue, South
New York, New York 10003
Tel: (212) 777-5752

Rochester – NCA-Rochester Area-
Health Association of Rochester
and Monroe County, Inc.
973 East Avenue
Rochester, New York 14607
Tel: (716) 271-3540

Utica – NCA-Oneida County, Inc.
167 Genesee Street
Utica, New York 13501
Tel: (315) 732-1072

White Plains – Westchester Council on
Alcoholism
129 Court Street
White Plains, New York 10601
Tel: (914) 946-1358

OHIO

Cincinnati — Council on Alcoholism of
the Cincinnati Area
2400 Reading Road - Room 202
Cincinnati, Ohio 45202
Tel: (513) 721-2905

OKLAHOMA

Tulsa — Tulsa Council on Alcoholism
2121 South Columbia Avenue
Suite LL 1, Parkland Plaza Building
Tulsa, Oklahoma 74114
Tel: (918) 747-8891

PENNSYLVANIA

Bethlehem — Bethlehem Council on
Alcoholism
Community Chest Building
520 East Broad Street
Bethlehem, Pennsylvania 18018
Tel: (215) 867-3986

Lancaster — NCA-Lancaster County,
Inc.
630 Janet Avenue
Lancaster, Pennsylvania 17601
Tel: (717) 299-2831

Philadelphia — NCA-Delaware Valley
Area, Inc.
3401 Market Street
Philadelphia, Pennsylvania 19104
Tel: (215) 387-0590

Pittsburgh — Alcoholism Program -
United Mental Health Services of
Allegheny County, Inc.
4026 Jenkins Arcade
Pittsburgh, Pennsylvania 15222
Tel: (412) 391-3820

Reading — NCA-Berks County, Inc.
300 North Fifth Street
Reading, Pennsylvania 19601
Tel: (215) 372-8917-18

RHODE ISLAND

Providence — "Hope" Council on
Alcoholism, Inc.
P.O. Box 2451
Providence, Rhode Island 02906
Tel: (401) 421-2027

TENNESSEE

Chattanooga — Chattanooga Area
Council on Alcoholism and Drug
Abuse
1212 Dodds Avenue
Chattanooga, Tennessee 37403
Tel: (615) 267-3354

Memphis — Memphis Alcohol and Drug
Council
1349 Monroe Avenue - Room 302
Memphis, Tennessee 38104
Tel: (901) 272-1757

Nashville — Mid-Cumberland
Council on Alcohol and
Drugs
814 Church Street
Nashville, Tennessee 37203
Tel: (615) 254-6547

TEXAS

Houston — Houston Council on
Alcoholism
601 Medical Towers
Houston, Texas 77025
Tel: (713) 526-1791

San Antonio — NCA-San Antonio Area
5307 Broadway - Suite 209
San Antonio, Texas 78209
Tel: (512) 828-3742

VIRGINIA

Norfolk — Virginia Council on
Alcoholism & Drug Dependence -
Tidewater Area
Suite 520 - Professional Arts Building
142 West York Street
Norfolk, Virginia 23510
Tel: (703) 625-5838

WASHINGTON

Seattle — Seattle-King County Council
on Alcoholism
3109 Arcade Building
1319 Second Avenue
Seattle, Washington 98101
Tel: (206) 623-8380

Vancouver — Clark County Council on
Alcoholism
207 Central Building
1206½ Main Street
Vancouver, Washington 98660
Tel: (206) 696-1631

Yakima — Yakima Valley Council on
Alcoholism
202 Miller Building
Yakima, Washington 98901
Tel: (509) 248-1800

WISCONSIN

Milwaukee — Milwaukee Council on
Alcoholism, Inc.
135 West Wells Street - Suite 416
Milwaukee, Wisconsin 53203
Tel: (414) 276-8487

ASSOCIATE DIRECTORY
March 1972

ALABAMA

Mobile — Southwest Alabama Council
on Alcoholism, Inc.
1950 Government Street - Room 202
Mobile, Alabama 36606
Tel: (205) 471-3977

ALASKA

Kodiak — Kodiak Council on
Alcoholism
P.O. Box 627
Kodiak, Alaska 99615

ARIZONA

Tucson — Alcoholism Council of
Southern Arizona
Box 4845, University Station
Tucson, Arizona 85717
Tel: (602) 325-6074

Yuma — Yuma County on Alcoholism
& Drug Abuse
2222 Avenue A, Wing D, Room 8
Yuma, Arizona 85364

CALIFORNIA

Placerville — El Dorado Council on
Alcoholism
P.O. Box 246
Placerville, California 95667

Riverside — Committee on Alcoholism
& Drug Abuse for Inland Empire
3701 Merrill Avenue
Riverside, California 92506
Tel: (714) 682-4644

San Luis Obispo — National Council on
Alcoholism San Luis Obispo Area,
Inc.
1987 Wilding Lane
San Luis Obispo, California 94301
Tel: (805) 543-2723

Santa Ana — Orange County Council
on Alcoholism
1913 East 17th Street - Suite 103
Santa Ana, California 92703
Tel: (714) 835-3830

Santa Rosa — Sonoma County Council
on Alcoholism
P.O. Box 2661
Santa Rosa, California 95404
Tel: (707) 544-7544

CONNECTICUT
Groton — Southeastern Council on
Alcoholism & Drug Dependence,
Inc.
242 North Road
P.O. Box 962
Groton, Connecticut 06340
Tel: (403) 455-8511

New Haven — The Alcohol Council of
Greater New Haven
412 Orange Street
New Haven, Connecticut 06511

FLORIDA
Fort Lauderdale — Broward County
Commission on Alcoholism
Bennett Building - Room 219
4 N. Federal Highway
Fort Lauderdale, Florida 33301
Tel: (305) 525-0206

Miami Beach — City of Miami Beach
Court Alcoholic Rehabilitation Program
1001 Ocean Drive
Miami Beach, Florida 33139

Sarasota — Sarasota Rehabilitation Program, Inc.
727 So. Orange Avenue
Sarasota, Florida 33577

GEORGIA
Waycross — Area Drug Alcoholism
Council
102 Gilmore Street
Waycross, Georgia 31501

ILLINOIS
Aurora — Mercyville Institute of
Mental Health
1330 No. Lake Street
Aurora, Illinois 60506

Peoria — Peoria Area Council on
Alcoholism
Allied Agencies Center
320 East Armstrong Avenue
Peoria, Illinois 61603
Tel: (309) 676-4681

INDIANA
South Bend — Alcoholism Council,
Inc. of St. Joseph County
521 W. Colfax Avenue
South Bend, Indiana 46601
Tel: (219) 234-3136

IOWA
Sioux City — Siouxland and Council
on Alcoholism
St. Vincent Hospital - Rooms 210 - 215
624 Jones Street
Sioux City, Iowa 51104
Tel: (712) 279-2123

KENTUCKY
Anchorage — Alcoholic Information
Center
9911 La Grange Road
Anchorage, Kentucky 40223

Harlan — Upper Cumberland and
Alcoholism & Drug Abuse Council,
Inc.
c/o Bank of Harlan
Box 919
Harlan, Kentucky 40831

LOUISIANA

Baton Rouge — Baton Rouge Area
Council on Alcoholism & Drug
Abuse
2035 Wooddale Blvd.
Suite E
Baton Rouge, Louisiana 70806
Tel: (504) 924-6630

Monroe — Twin Cities Council on
Alcoholism
P.O. Box 332
2400 Louisville Avenue
Monroe, Louisiana 71201
Tel: (318) 323-0231

MARYLAND

Easton — Eastern Shore Council on
Alcoholism, Inc.
P.O. Box 351
Easton, Maryland 21601
Tel: (301) 822-4133

Hagerstown — Washington County
Council on Alcoholism
310 Professional Arts Bldg.
Hagerstown, Maryland 21740

MASSACHUSETTS

Salem — North Shore Committee on
Alcoholism, Inc.
5 Broad Street, Health Center
Salem, Massachusetts 01970

Worcester — Worcester County Council
on Alcoholism, Inc.
9 Walnut Street
Worcester, Massachusetts
Tel: (617) 757-1423

MICHIGAN

Ann Arbor — The Washtenaw County
Council on Alcoholism
218 North Division Street
Ann Arbor, Michigan 48106
Tel: (313) 971-7900

Kalamazoo Alcoholism and
Addiction Council
350 South Burdick Street
Kalamazoo, Michigan 49001
Tel: (616) 381-6642

Munising — Alger County Alcoholism
Council
Box 87
Munising, Michigan 49862
Tel: (906) 387-3210

MINNESOTA

Minneapolis — Minnesota Council on
Alcohol Problems
122 West Franklin Avenue
Minneapolis, Minnesota 55404

Minneapolis — Lynnville, Inc.
230 Oak Grove
Minneapolis, Minnesota 55403

MISSISSIPPI

Parchman — Department of Alcoholic
Rehabilitation
Mississippi State Penitentiary
Parchman, Mississippi 38738
Tel: (601) 745-2411

NEBRASKA

Grand Island — Central Nebraska
Council on Alcoholism
208 Masonic Building
Grand Island, Nebraska 68801
Tel: (308) 384-7365

NEVADA

Las Vegas — Southern Nevada
Council on Alcoholism
13 Harvard Street
Las Vegas, Nevada 89107
Tel: (702) 384-9009

NEW JERSEY
Burlington — Burlington County
  Community Action Program
9 West Union Street
Burlington, New Jersey 08016

Flemington — Hunterdon Council on
  Alcoholism
c/o Hunterdon Medical Center
Flemington, New Jersey 08822

NEW YORK
Ithaca — Alcoholism Council of
  Tompkins County
223 Fayette Street
Ithaca, New York 14850

Johnson City — Broome County
  Committee on Alcoholism, Inc.
44 Harrison Street
Johnson City, New York 13790
Tel: (607) 798-9971

Niagara Falls — Niagara County
  Council on Alcoholism, Inc.
727 Main Street
Niagara Falls, New York
Tel: (716) 282-1002

Saranac Lake — St. Joseph's Rehabili-
  tation Center
P.O. Box 470
Saranac Lake, New York 12983
Tel: (518) 891-3950

Schenectady — Alcoholism Council of
  Schenectady County, Inc.
277 State Street
Schenectady, New York 12305
Tel: (518) 372-3371

Syracuse — Onodaga Council on
  Alcoholism
Community Chest Building - Room 405
107 James Street
Syracuse, New York 13202
Tel: (315) 471-1359

Watertown — Jefferson County
  Committee on Alcoholism, Inc.
Hotel Woodruff - Suite 118
Watertown, New York 13601

NORTH CAROLINA
Charlotte — Charlotte Council on
  Alcoholism, Inc.
100 Billingsley Road
Charlotte, North Carolina 28211
Tel: (704) 375-5521

Durham — Durham Council on
  Alcoholism
606 Snow Building
Durham, North Carolina 27701
Tel: (919) 682-5227

Morganton — Burke County Council on
  Alcoholism, Inc.
211 North Sterling Street
Morganton, North Carolina 28655
Tel: (704) 433-1221

OHIO
Hamilton — NCA-Butler County, Inc.
Gonzaga Memorial Hall
Mercy Hospital
111 Buckeye Street
Hamilton, Ohio 45011
Tel: (513) 869-6471

OREGON
Portland — Council on Alcoholism
  Portland Tri-County Area
538 S. E. Ash
Portland, Oregon 97214
Tel: (503) 255-6649

PENNSYLVANIA

Allentown — Lehigh County Council on Alcohol and Drug Abuse
34 North Fifth Street
Allentown, Pennsylvania 18101
Tel: (215) 437-0801

Erie — Erie Council on Alcoholism
110 West 10th Street
Erie, Pennsylvania 16501

Johnstown — Conemaugh Valley Council on Alcoholism
418 Lincoln Street
Johnstown, Pennsylvania 15906
Tel: (814) 535-6211

Pittsburgh — Community Action Pittsburgh, Inc.
107 Sixth Street
Pittsburgh, Pennsylvania 15222
Tel: (412) 355-6333

Scranton — Alcoholism & Drug Abuse Council of Northeastern Pennsylvania
Suite 404 - Chamber of Commerce Building
Scranton, Pennsylvania 18503
Tel: (717) 346-7309

Washington — Washington County Council on Alcoholism, Inc.
18 West Wheeling Street
Washington, Pennsylvania 15301
Tel: (412) 222-7150

SOUTH CAROLINA

Charleston — Trident Council on Alcohol & Drug Abuse
P.O. Box 2682
Charleston, South Carolina 29403

TEXAS

Austin — Austin Council on Alcoholism
411 Littlefield Building
Austin, Texas 78701
Tel: (512) 472-2461

Orange — Orange Council on Alcoholism
P.O. Box 635
408 North 5th Street
Orange, Texas 77630
Tel: (713) 883-4532

VIRGINIA

Abingdon — The Progressive Community Club
118 Wall Street
Abingdon, Virginia 24210

Richmond — The Middle Atlantic Institute for Alcohol and other Drug Studies
3202 W. Cary Street
Richmond, Virginia 23221

WASHINGTON

Longview — Lower Columbia Council on Alcoholism
835 15th Avenue
Longview, Washington 98632

Olympia — Thurston-Mason Counties, Inc. Alcoholism Information & Referral Center
110 West State Street
Olympia, Washington 98501
Tel: (206) 943-8510

Seattle — The Studio Club
9010 13th Avenue N.W.
Seattle, Washington 98107

Tacoma — Pierce County Council on
    Alcoholism
109 North Tacoma Avenue
Tacoma, Washington 98403
Tel: (206) 383-3311 ext. 761

WISCONSIN

Baldwin — Tri-County Council on
    Alcohol-Drug Abuse
Box 64
Baldwin, Wisconsin 54002

Kenosha — Kenosha County Council on
    Alcoholism
16-17 Isermann Building
616 56th Street
Kenosha, Wisconsin 53140

Green Bay — Brown County
    Educational & Information
    Center on Alcoholism
Room 300 - Courthouse Annex
Green Bay, Wisconsin 54301
Tel: (414) 432-1959

La Crosse — West Central Council on
    Alcoholism
1312 Winnebago Street
La Crosse, Wisconsin 54601

PUBLIC LAW 91-616

Public Law 91-616
91st Congress, S. 3835
December 31, 1970

An Act

84 STAT. 1848

To provide a comprehensive Federal program for the prevention and treatment of alcohol abuse and alcoholism.

Be it enacted by the Senate and House of Representatives of the United States of America in Congress assembled,

Comprehensive
Alcohol Abuse
and Alcoholism
Prevention,
Treatment, and
Rehabilitation
Act of 1970.

SHORT TITLE

Section 1. This Act may be cited as the "Comprehensive Alcohol Abuse and Alcoholism Prevention, Treatment, and Rehabilitation Act of 1970".

TITLE I—NATIONAL INSTITUTE ON ALCOHOL ABUSE AND ALCOHOLISM

ESTABLISHMENT OF THE INSTITUTE

Sec. 101. (a) There is established in the National Institute of Mental Health, the National Institute on Alcohol Abuse and Alcoholism (hereafter in this Act referred to as the "Institute") to administer the programs and authorities assigned to the Secretary of Health, Education, and Welfare (hereafter in this Act referred to as the "Secretary") by this Act and part C of the Community Mental Health Centers Act. The Secretary, acting through the Institute, shall, in carrying out the purposes of section 301 of the Public Health Service Act with respect to alcohol abuse and alcoholism, develop and conduct comprehensive health, education, training, research, and planning programs for the prevention and treatment of alcohol abuse and alcoholism and for the rehabilitation of alcohol abusers and alcoholics.

82 Stat. 1006;
Ante, p. 59.
42 USC 2688e.
58 Stat. 691;
79 Stat. 448.
42 USC 241.

(b) The Institute shall be under the direction of a Director who shall be appointed by the Secretary.

REPORTS BY THE SECRETARY

Sec. 102. The Secretary shall—

(1) submit an annual report to Congress which shall include a description of the actions taken, services provided, and funds expended under this Act and part C of the Community Mental Health Centers Act, an evaluation of the effectiveness of such actions, services, and expenditures of funds, and such other information as the Secretary considers appropriate;

Reports to
President and
Congress.

131

84 STAT. 1849

(2) submit to Congress on or before the expiration of the one-year period beginning on the date of enactment of this Act a report (A) containing current information on the health consequences of using alcoholic beverages, and (B) containing such recommendations for legislation and administrative action as he may deem appropriate;

(3) submit such additional reports as may be requested by the President of the United States or by Congress; and

(4) submit to the President of the United States and to Congress such recommendations as will further the prevention, treatment, and control of alcohol abuse and alcoholism.

TITLE II—ALCOHOL ABUSE AND ALCOHOLISM PREVENTION, TREATMENT, AND REHABILITATION PROGRAMS FOR FEDERAL CIVILIAN EMPLOYEES

ALCOHOL ABUSE AND ALCOHOLISM AMONG FEDERAL CIVILIAN EMPLOYEES

Sec. 201. (a) The Civil Service Commission shall be responsible for developing and maintaining, in cooperation with the Secretary and with other Federal agencies and departments, appropriate prevention, treatment, and rehabilitation programs and services for alcohol abuse and alcoholism among Federal civilian employees, consistent with the purposes of this Act. Such policies and services shall make optimal use of existing governmental facilities, services, and skills.

(b) The Secretary, acting through the Institute, shall be responsible for fostering similar alcohol abuse and alcoholism prevention, treatment, and rehabilitation programs and services in State and local governments and in private industry.

(c) (1) No person may be denied or deprived of Federal civilian employment or a Federal professional or other license or right solely on the ground of prior alcohol abuse or prior alcoholism.

(2) This subsection shall not apply to employment (A) in the Central Intelligence Agency, the Federal Bureau of Investigation, the National Security Agency, or any other department or agency of the Federal Government designated for purposes of national

84 STAT. 1850

security by the President, or (B) in any position in any department or agency of the Federal Government, not referred to in clause (A), which position is determined pursuant to regulations prescribed by the head of such agency or department to be a sensitive position.

(d) This title shall not be construed to prohibit the dismissal from employment of a Federal civilian employee who cannot properly function in his employment.

TITLE III—FEDERAL ASSISTANCE FOR STATE AND LOCAL PROGRAMS

PART A—FORMULA GRANTS

AUTHORIZATION

Sec. 301. There are authorized to be appropriated $40,000,000 for the fiscal year ending June 30, 1971, $60,000,000 for the fiscal year ending June 30, 1972, $80,000,000 for the fiscal year ending June 30, 1973, for grants to States to assist them in planning, establishing, maintaining, coordinating, and evaluating projects for the development of more effective prevention, treatment, and rehabilitation programs to deal with alcohol abuse and alcoholism. For purposes of this part, the term "State" includes the District of Columbia, the Virgin Islands, the Commonwealth of Puerto Rico, Guam, American Samoa, and the Trust Territory of the Pacific Islands, in addition to the fifty States.

Appropriation.

"State."

STATE ALLOTMENT

Sec. 302. (a) For each fiscal year the Secretary shall, in accordance with regulations, allot the sums appropriated for such year pursuant to section 301 among the States on the basis of the relative population, financial need, and need for more effective prevention, treatment, and rehabilitation of alcohol abuse and alcoholism; except that no such allotment to any State (other than the Virgin Islands, American Samoa, Guam, and the Trust Territory of the Pacific Islands) for any fiscal year shall be less than $200,000.

(b) Any amount so allotted to a State (other than the Virgin Islands, American Samoa, Guam, and the Trust Territory of the

84 STAT. 1851

Pacific Islands) and remaining unobligated at the end of such year shall remain available to such State, for the purposes for which made, for the next fiscal year (and for such year only), and any such amount shall be in addition to the amounts allotted to such State for such purpose for such next fiscal year; except that any such amount, remaining unobligated at the end of the sixth month following the end of such year for which it was allotted, which the Secretary determines will remain unobligated by the close of such next fiscal year, may be reallotted by the Secretary, to be available for the purposes for which made until the close of such next fiscal year, to other States which have need therefor, on such basis as the Secretary deems equitable and consistent with the purposes of this part, and any amount so reallotted to a State shall be in addition to the amounts allotted and available to the States for the same period. Any amount allotted under subsection (a) to the Virgin Islands, American Samoa, Guam, or the Trust Territory of the Pacific Islands for a fiscal year and remaining unobligated at the end of such year shall remain available to it, for the purposes for which made, for the next two fiscal years (and for such years only), and any such amount shall be in addition to the amounts allotted to it for such purpose for each of such next two fiscal years; except that any such amount, remaining unobligated at the end of the first of such next two years, which the Secretary determines will remain unobligated at the close of the second of such next two years, to any other of such four States which have need therefor, on such basis as the Secretary deems equitable and consistent with the purposes of this part, and any amount so reallotted to a State shall be in addition to the amounts allotted and available to the State for the same period.

(c) At the request of any State, a portion of any allotment or allotments of such State under this part shall be available to pay that portion of the expenditures found necessary by the Secretary for the proper and efficient administration during such year of the State plan approved under this part, except that not more than 10 per centum of the total of the allotments of such State ιor a year, or $50,000, whichever is the least, shall be available for such purpose for such year.

December 31, 1970   Pub. Law 91-616

84 STAT. 1852

STATE PLANS

Sec. 303. (a) Any State desiring to participate in this part shall submit a State plan for carrying out its purposes. Such plan must—

(1) designate a single State agency as the sole agency for the administration of the plan, or designate such agency as the sole agency for supervising the administration of the plan;

(2) contain satisfactory evidence that the State agency designated in accordance with paragraph (1) (hereafter in this section referred to as the "State agency") will have authority to carry out such plan in conformity with this part;

(3) provide for the designation of a State advisory council which shall include representatives of nongovernmental organizations or groups, and of public agencies concerned with the prevention and treatment of alcohol abuse and alcoholism, to consult with the State agency in carrying out the plan;

(4) set forth, in accordance with criteria established by the Secretary, a survey of need for the prevention and treatment of alcohol abuse and alcoholism including a survey of the health facilities needed to provide services for alcohol abuse and alcoholism and a plan for the development and distribution of such facilities and programs throughout the State;

(5) provide such methods of administration of the State plan, including methods relating to the establishment and maintenance of personnel standards on a merit basis (except that the Secretary shall exercise no authority with respect to the selection, tenure of office, or compensation of any individual employed in accordance with such methods), as are found by the Secretary to be necessary for the proper and efficient operation of the plan;

(6) provide that the State agency will make such reports, in such form and containing such information, as the Secretary may from time to time reasonably require, and will keep such records and afford such access thereto as the Secretary may find necessary to assure the correctness and verification of such reports;

(7) provide that the Comptroller General of the United

84 STAT. 1853

States or his duly authorized representatives shall have access for the purpose of audit and examination to the records specified in paragraph (6);

(8) provide that the State agency will from time to time, but not less often than annually, review its State plan and submit to the Secretary any modifications thereof which it considers necessary;

(9) provide reasonable assurance that Federal funds made available under this part for any period will be so used as to supplement and increase, to the extent feasible and practical, the level of State, local, and other non-Federal funds that would in the absence of such Federal funds be made available for the programs described in this part, and will in no event supplant such State, local, and other non-Federal funds; and

(10) contain such additional information and assurance as the Secretary may find necessary to carry out the provisions and purposes of this part.

State plans, approval.

(b) The Secretary shall approve any State plan and any modification thereof which complies with the provisions of subsection

PART B–PROJECT GRANTS AND CONTRACTS

GRANTS AND CONTRACTS FOR THE PREVENTION AND TREATMENT OF ALCOHOL ABUSE AND ALCOHOLISM

80 Stat. 1009;
Ante, p. 59.
42 USC 2688e
note.

Sec. 311. Section 247 of part C of the Community Mental Health Centers Act is amended to read as follows:

"GRANTS AND CONTRACTS FOR THE PREVENTION AND TREATMENT OF ALCOHOL ABUSE AND ALCOHOLISM

"Sec. 247. (a) The Secretary, acting through the National Institute on Alcohol Abuse and Alcoholism, may make grants to public and private nonprofit agencies, organizations, and institutions and may enter into contracts with public and private agencies, organizations, and institutions, and individuals—

"(1) to conduct demonstration, service, and evaluation projects,

"(2) to provide education and training,

"(3) to provide programs and services in cooperation with schools, courts, penal institutions, and other public agencies, and

"(4) to provide counseling and education activities on an

December 31, 1970   Pub. Law 91-616

84 STAT. 1854

individual or community basis, for the prevention and treatment of alcohol abuse and alcoholism and for the rehabilitation of alcohol abusers and alcoholics.

"(b) Projects for which grants or contracts are made under this section shall, whenever possible, be community based, provide a comprehensive range of services, and be integrated with, and involve the active participation of, a wide range of public and nongovernmental agencies, organizations, institutions, and individuals.

"(c) (1) In administering the provisions of this section, the Secretary shall require coordination of all applications for programs in a State.

Applications.

"(2) Each applicant from within a State, upon filing its application with the Secretary for a grant or contract under this section, shall submit a copy of its application for review by the State agency designated under section 303 of the Comprehensive Alcohol Abuse and Alcoholism Prevention, Treatment, and Rehabilitation Act of 1970, if such agency exists. Such State agency shall be g iven not more than thirty days from the date of receipt of the application to submit to the Secretary, in writing, an evaluation of the project set forth in the application. Such evaluation shall include comments on the relationship of the project to other projects pending and approved and to the State comprehensive plan for treatment and prevention of alcohol abuse and alcoholism under such section 303. The State shall furnish the applicant a copy of any such evaluation.

Filing.

Ante, p. 1850.

"(3) Approval of any application for a grant or contract by the Secretary, including the earmarking of financial assistance for a program or project, may be granted only if the application substantially meets a set of criteria established by the Secretary that—

Approval, criteria.

"(A) provide that the activities and services for which assistance under this section is sought will be substantially administered by or under the supervision of the applicant;

"(B) provide for such methods of administration as are necessary for the proper and efficient operation of such programs or projects;

"(C) provide for such fiscal control and fund accounting procedures as may be necessary to assure proper disbursement

138

Pub. Law 91-616   December 31, 1970

84 STAT. 1855

of and accounting for Federal funds paid to the applicant; and

"(D) provide reasonable assurance that Federal funds made available under this section for any period will be so used as to supplement and increase, to the extent feasible and practical, the level of State, local, and other non-Federal funds that would in the absence of such Federal funds be made available for the programs described in this section, and will in no event supplant such State, local, and other non-Federal funds.

Appropriation.

"(d) To carry out the purposes of this section, there are authorized to be appropriated $30,000,000 for the fiscal year ending June 30, 1971, $40,000,000 for the fiscal year ending June 30, 1972, and $50,000,000 for the fiscal year ending June 30, 1973."

PART C—ADMISSION TO HOSPITALS

ADMISSION OF ALCOHOL ABUSERS AND ALCOHOLICS TO PRIVATE AND PUBLIC HOSPITALS

Failure to comply, termination of Federal assistance.

Sec. 321. (a) Alcohol abusers and alcoholics shall be admitted to and treated in private and public general hospitals, which receive Federal funds for alcoholic treatment programs, on the basis of medical need and shall not be discriminated against solely because of their alcoholism. No hospital that violates this section shall receive Federal financial assistance under the provisions of this Act; except that the Secretary shall not terminate any such Federal assistance until the Secretary has advised the appropriate person or persons of the failure to comply with this section, and has provided an opportunity for correction or a hearing.

Hearing opportunity. Judicial review.

77 Stat. 298. 42 USC 2694,

(b) Any action taken by the Secretary pursuant to this section shall be subject to such judicial review as is provided by section 404 of the Community Mental Health Centers Act.

PART D—GENERAL

COMPREHENSIVE STATE HEALTH PLANS

80 Stat. 1184; Ante, p. 1241. 42 USC 246.

Sec. 331. Section 314(d) (2) of the Public Health Service Act is amended—

(1) by striking out "and" at the end of subparagraph (J);

(2) by striking out the period at the end of subparagraph (K) and inserting in lieu thereof "; and"; and

(3) by adding after subparagraph (K) the following new subparagraph:

"(L) provide for services for the prevention and treatment of alcohol abuse and alcoholism, commensurate with the extent of the problem."

SPECIALIZED FACILITIES

Sec. 332. Section 243(a) of the Community Mental Health Centers Act is amended (1) by inserting "or leasing" after "construction", and (2) by inserting "facilities for emergency medical services, intermediate care services, or outpatient services, and" immediately before "post-hospitalization treatment facilities".

82 Stat. 1008
42 USC 2688h.

CONFIDENTIALITY OF RECORDS

Sec. 333. The Secretary may authorize persons engaged in research on, or treatment with respect to, alcohol abuse and alcoholism to protect the privacy of individuals who are the subject of such research or treatment by withholding from all persons not connected with the conduct of such research or treatment the names or other identifying characteristics of such individuals. Persons so authorized to protect the privacy of such individuals may not be compelled in any Federal, State, or local civil, criminal, administrative, legislative, or other proceeding to indentify such individuals.

Research and treatment populations.

TITLE IV—THE NATIONAL ADVISORY COUNCIL ON ALCOHOL ABUSE AND ALCOHOLISM

ESTABLISHMENT OF COUNCIL

Sec. 401. (a) Section 217(a) of the Public Health Service Act is amended—

64 Stat. 446.
42 USC 218.

(1) in the first sentence thereof, by inserting "the National Advisory Council on Alcohol Abuse and Alcoholism," immediately after "the National Advisory Mental Health Council,";

(2) in the second sentence thereof, by (A) inserting "the National Advisory Council on Alcoholic Abuse and Alcoholism," immediately after "the National Advisory Mental Health Council,", and (B) inserting "alcohol abuse and alcoholism," immediately after "psychiatric disorders,"; and

(3) in the fourth sentence, (A) by inserting "(other than the members of the National Advisory Council on Alcohol Abuse and Alcoholism)" after "the terms of the members"; (B) by striking out "and" before "(2)"; and (C) by striking out the period at the end and inserting a semicolon and "and (3) the

terms of the members of the National Council on Alcohol Abuse and Alcoholism first taking office after the date of enactment of this clause, shall expire as follows: Three shall expire four years after such date, three shall expire three years after such date, three shall expire two years after such date, and three shall expire one year after such date, as designated by the Secretary at the time of appointment."

64 Stat. 446.
42 USC 218.

(b) Section 217(b) of such Act is amended, in the second sentence thereof, by inserting "alcohol abuse and alcoholism," immediately after "mental health,".

(c) Section 217 of such Act is further amended by adding at the end thereof the following new subsection:

"(d) The National Advisory Council on Alcohol Abuse and Alcoholism shall advise, consult with, and make recommendations to, the Secretary on matters relating to the activities and functions of the Secretary in the field of alcohol abuse and alcoholism. The Council is authorized (1) to review research projects or programs submitted to or initiated by it in the field of alcohol abuse and alcoholism and recommend to the Secretary any such projects which it believes show promise of making valuable contributions to human knowledge with respect to the cause, prevention, or methods of diagnosis and treatment of alcohol abuse and alcoholism, and (2) to collect information as to studies being carried on in the field of alcohol abuse and alcoholism and, with the approval of the Secretary, make available such information through appropriate publications for the benefit of health and welfare agencies or organizations (public or private) or physicians or any other scientists, and for the information of

58 Stat. 709.
42 USC 219.

the general public. The Council is also authorized to recommend to the Secretary, for acceptance pursuant to section 501 of this Act, conditional gifts for work in the field of alcohol abuse and alcoholism; and the Secretary shall recommend acceptance of any such gifts only after consultation with the Council."

APPROVAL BY COUNCIL OF CERTAIN GRANTS UNDER PART C OF
COMMUNITY MENTAL HEALTH CENTERS ACT

Ante, p. 62.

Sec. 402. Section 266 of the Community Mental Health Centers Act is amended (1) by inserting "(other than part C thereof)" immediately after "this title", and (2) by adding immediately after the period the following: "Grants under part C of this title for such costs may be made only upon recommendation of the National Advisory Council on Alcohol Abuse and Alcoholism established by such section."

TITLE V—GENERAL

Sec. 501. If any section, provision, or term of this Act is adjudged invalid for any reason, such judgment shall not affect, impair, or invalidate any other section, provision, or term of this Act, and the remaining sections, provisions, and terms shall be and remain in full force and effect.   **Separability.**

Sec. 502. (a) Each recipient of assistance under this Act pursuant to grants or contracts entered into under other than competitive bidding procedures shall keep such records as the Secretary shall prescribe, including records which fully disclose the amount and disposition by such recipient of the proceeds of such grant or contract, the total cost of the project or undertaking in connection with which such grant or contract is given or used, and the amount of that portion of the cost of the project or undertaking supplied by other sources, and such other records as will facilitate an effective audit.   **Recordkeeping.**

(b) The Secretary and Comptroller General of the United States, or any of their duly authorized representatives, shall have access for the purpose of audit and examination to any books, documents, papers, and records of such recipients that are pertinent to the grants or contracts entered into under the provisions of this Act under other than competitive bidding procedures.   **Records, accessibility.**

Sec. 503. Payments under this Act may be made in advance or by way of reimbursement and in such installments as the Secretary may determine.   **Payments**

Approved December 31, 1970.

LEGISLATIVE HISTORY:

HOUSE REPORT No. 91-1663 accompanying H. R. 18874 (Comm. on Interstate and Foreign Commerce).
SENATE REPORT No. 91-1069 (Comm. on Labor and Public Welfare).
CONGRESSIONAL RECORD, Vol. 116 (1970):
    Aug. 10, considered and passed Senate.
    Dec. 18, considered and passed House, amended, in lieu of H.R. 18874.
    Dec. 19, Senate agreed to House amendment.

AL-ANON AND ALATEEN
CONFERENCE APPROVED LITERATURE

(May be ordered from Al-Anon Family Group Headquarters, Inc., P. O. Box 182, Madison Square Station, New York, New York 10010.)

BOOKS

Al-Anon Faces Alcoholism. A book for everyone concerned with the problem. Includes articles by outstanding professionals in the field and personal histories that detail a wide variety of situations. Al-Anon principles are made clear through analyses of the Slogans. The final section is a history of the fellowship from the early days. $5.50

Al-Anon's Favorite Forum Editorials. Material selected from issues of *The Forum* published from 1954 to 1970. $5.50

Alateen—Hope for Children of Alcoholics. The history of Alateen; understanding alcoholism; the steps, traditions, and slogans; personal stories; the structure of Alateen; and more; written by Alateens. $3.50

The Dilemma of the Alcoholic Marriage. $4.50

Living with an Alcoholic. The history and purposes of the fellowship, how it works, how it is held in unity; with stories by husbands, wives, parents, and offspring of those who suffer from alcoholism. $4.50

One Day at a Time in Al-Anon. Inspirational daily readings about the Al-Anon philosophy and how it can be used in daily life. $4.00

MONTHLY PUBLICATION

Al-Anon Family Group Forum. Articles, letters, meeting ideas, inspiration, and encouragement. Subscriptions: 1 year, $2.50; 2 years, $4.50

BOOKLETS AND LEAFLETS

LEARNING ABOUT AL-ANON

Al-Anon, You and the Alcoholic. Answers to questions about how Al-Anon helps families to deal with problems. 16-page booklet, 15¢

Freedom from Despair. 4-page leaflet, 5¢

Information for the Newcomer. Brief, concise explanation of Al-Anon. Printed sheet, 5¢

Jane's Husband Drank Too Much. Cartoon booklet depicting typical Al-Anon story. 15¢

Lois's Story: Al-Anon from the Beginning. Dramatic story of Al-Anon founder. 8-page leaflet, 10¢

Purposes and Suggestions. Aims of the Al-Anon program and ideas for those in need of help. 6-panel leaflet, 5¢

So You Love an Alcoholic. First steps to a changed attitude toward the alcoholic. 6-panel leaflet, 5¢

This Is Al-Anon. Basics on Al-Anon ideas and working tools. 16-page booklet, 15¢

What Do You Do about the Alcoholic's Drinking? Shows errors most make in trying to cope with the alcoholic problem. 12-page booklet, 10¢

FOR FURTHER STUDY

Alcoholism, A Merry-Go-Round Named Denial. 18-page
    booklet, 20¢
Alcoholism, the Family Disease. 48-page brochure, 25¢
A Guide for the Family of the Alcoholic. 16-page booklet, 10¢
How to Know an Alcoholic. 16-page pamphlet, 30¢
The Twelve Steps and Traditions. 32 pages, 25¢
Three Views of Al-Anon. 8-page booklet, 10¢
Why Is Al-Anon Anonymous? 16-page booklet, 15¢

AL-ANON FOR MEN

Al-Anon Is for Men. 8-page booklet, 10¢
"My Wife Drinks Too Much." 16-page booklet, 15¢
What's Next? Asks the Husband of an Alcoholic. 16-page
    booklet, 15¢

FOR PARENTS

How Can I Help My Children? Asks an Al-Anon Member.
    20-page booklet, 15¢
To the Mother and Father of an Alcoholic. 8-page booklet,
    15¢

ALATEEN

If Your Parents Drink Too Much. 15¢
It's A Teenaged Affair. 4-page leaflet, 5¢
Operation Alateen. 8-page leaflet, 10¢
Twelve Steps and Twelve Traditions for Alateen. 56-page
    booklet, 35¢
Youth and the Alcoholic Parent. 14-page booklet, 15¢

FOR RELATIVES OF ALCOHOLICS IN INSTITUTIONS

Homeward Bound. 16-page booklet, 10¢

SPONSORSHIP

A Guide for Sponsors of Alateen Groups. 6-panel folder, 10¢
Sponsorship: What It's All About. 12-page booklet, 15¢

BIBLIOGRAPHY

Addeo, Edmond, and Addeo, Jovita R. *Why Our Children Drink*. Englewood Cliffs, N.J.: Prentice-Hall, 1975.

Alcohol and Health. Report from the Secretary of Health, Education and Welfare. New York: Charles Scribner's Sons, 1970.

Alfars, Albert L., and Milgram, Gail. *The Teenager and Alcohol*. New York: Rosen, Richards, Press, 1970.

Asbury, Herbert. *The Great Illusion, an Informal History of Prohibition*. Garden City, N.Y.: Doubleday & Co., 1950.

Brasch, R. *How Did It Begin?* New York: David McKay Co., 1965.

Brecher, Edward M., and the editors of *Consumers Reports. Licit and Illicit Drugs*. Boston: Little, Brown and Company, 1972.

Burgess, Louise Bailey. *Alcohol and Your Health*. Los Angeles: Charles Publishing Co., 1973.

Carroll, Charles R. *Alcohol: Use, Non-Use, and Abuse*. Dubuque, Iowa: William C. Brown Co., 1970.

Christopher D. Smithers Foundation, Inc. *Understanding Alcoholism*. New York: Charles Scribner's Sons, 1968.

Conley, Paul C., and Sorensen, Andrew A. *The Staggering Steeple*. Philadelphia: Pilgrim Press, 1971.

147

Cooperative Commission on the Study of Alcoholism. *Alcohol Problems—A Report to the Nation.* New York: Oxford University Press, 1967.

Cordasco, Francesco, ed. *Jacob Riis Revisited: Poverty and the Slum in Another Era.* New York: Doubleday & Co., 1968.

Drinking Game and How to Beat It, The. New York: Simon & Schuster, 1968.

"Drinking and 13-Year-Olds," *New York State Teacher,* 8 February 1976.

Emerson, Edward Randolph. *Beverages, Past and Present.* New York: G. P. Putnam's Sons, 1908.

Fort, Joel. *Alcohol: Our Biggest Drug Problem.* New York: McGraw-Hill Book Co., 1973.

Furnas, J. C. *The Life and Times of the Late Demon Rum.* New York: G. P. Putnam's Sons, 1965.

Gosher, Charles E. *Drinks, Drugs, Do-Gooders.* New York: Macmillan Co., The Free Press, 1973.

Hackwood, Frederick W. *Inns, Ales and Drinking Customs of Old England.* New York: Sturgiss & Walton Co., 1909.

Handlin, Oscar, and Handlin, Mary F. *Facing Life: Youth and the Family in American History.* Boston: Little, Brown & Co., 1971.

Hoffman, Frederick C. *A Handbook on Drug and Alcohol Abuse.* New York: Oxford University Press, 1975.

Hyde, Margaret. *Mind Drugs.* New York: McGraw-Hill Book Co., 1968.

Jellnick, E. M. *The Disease Concept of Alcoholism.* Highland Park, N.J.: Hillhouse Press, 1960.

Jones, Ben Morgan, and Parsons, Oscar A. "Getting High, Coming Down." *Psychology Today,* January 1975, pp. 53–58.

Maddox, George L., and McCall, Bevoda C. *Drinking Among*

Teenagers. New Brunswick, N.J.: Publication Division, Rutgers Center for Alcohol Studies, 1964.

Merv Griffin Show, The. "Teenage Alcoholism." WNEW-TV, December 12, 1974.

Null, Gary. *Body Pollution.* New York: Arco Publishing Co., Inc., 1973.

Phillipson, Richard V., ed. *Modern Trends in Drug Dependence and Alcoholism.* London: Butterworth & Co., 1970.

Roueché, Berton. *The Neutral Spirit.* Boston: Little, Brown & Co., 1960.

"School Study Calls 28% of Teen-Agers 'Problem' Drinkers," *The New York Times,* November 21, 1975.

Sinclair, Andrew. *Prohibition: The Era of Excess.* Boston: Little, Brown & Co., 1962.

Smith, W. H., and Smith, Helwig F. C. *Liquor, the Servant of Man.* Boston: Little, Brown & Co., 1939.

Stevenson, Burton, ed. *The Macmillan Book of Proverbs, Maxims and Famous Phrases.* New York: Macmillan Publishing Co., 1965.

Thompson, William A. R., M.D. *The Macmillan Medical Cyclopedia.* New York: Macmillan Publishing Co., 1959.

Whitney, Elizabeth D. *The Lonely Sickness.* Boston: Beacon Press, 1965.

Wilhelm, Richard, and Baynes, Carey F., trans. *The I Ching, or Book of Changes.* Princeton, N.J.: Princeton University Press, 1970.

INDEX